WE ARE THE DREAM

The Seven Seeds of American
Democracy

In Alliance with Civil Society in
Times of Uncertainty

Richard N. Hough
and
Dr. Frederick J.O. Ighoavodha Ph.D.

www.koanpublishing.com or 360-500-0550.

First Edition, Koan Publishing.

Library of Congress Card Catalog No.: 2008929845

ISBN: 978-0-9818688-0-6

Printed in the United States of America

DEDICATION

We all know there is a higher power: An unseen dimension that acts through all of us, connecting all of us. Our forefathers were clear on this; they spoke openly of it, and often. It is interwoven throughout our Constitution and the democracy it represents.

This is not a religious statement but a fact of spirit we are all blessed with. This book is dedicated to this spirit, its power, we all share and its uniqueness each one of us expresses.

This is the gift of life. This is our gift to life. When freely shared and freely honored, the beauty of life blossoms and prosperity flourishes.

As our consciousness changes and is acted upon, being freely expressed, our world changes. The dream becomes real. We are the dream. Wow...what a dream!

FORMAT

This is a different format. The type is larger so that it becomes an easy read, easy to highlight and easy to scan later. The margins are larger so you can easily write notes as needed. It is your book and meant to be used.

Although it could be used as a reference book, a text book, as well as a non-fiction book, none of these formats are effective. It is closely related to the format of a speaker. This enables the reader to step into the book and directly participate with it.

In short, you become the book, because, who you are interweaves between the lines; allowing your consciousness to awaken, enlivening and enhancing the words to who you are.

TABLE OF CONTENTS

TABLE OF CONTENTS, CONT'D.

PREFACE

We are certainly in times of uncertainty; not only at home here in America, but in all corners of the world. A commonality to us all, whether it be the environment, global warming or war. Economic, religious, political and social oppression once again rears its head and threatens the liberty and freedom of all, just as it did in the early 1600's, causing the **great migration** to the shores of an uncharted country.

Many people from different cultures, different backgrounds, different political and different religious beliefs came together and united in **common cause**. The individual, his **liberty** and **freedom** were once again important. American democracy was born. The "I" in the "We" were its core. The seeds had been planted. Life was on the move.

However, by 1776 life had deteriorated; greed and power had brought a new wave of oppression. The people speaking the sentiments of Patrick Henry "Give me liberty or give me death" (see pp. 17) united in **common cause** and revolted. The "I" in "We" had spoken. Liberty and freedom could not be defeated. American democracy was officially born and based on "We the people" where every **individual** was important; never to be expensed out. The "American Dream" was growing.

Today, we once again face the greed and power of a few with the oppression of the many. Our forefathers pointed out the dangers of our humanness with its need for personal power, always coming at the expense of others in the process, slowly eroding **freedom** and **liberty**, and the elimination of the individual. They had no solution that could be regulated by law. It was left up to the integrity of the people and its administrators.

What do we do today? Can we go back; ignite the passion of democracy, its **liberty** and **freedom**, and reclaim tomorrow, today? What is the role of the people in today's society? What happened? What needs to be done? How can we do it?

Can civil society and its organizations be neutral in keeping the public well informed, so that no group will ever have the power at the expense of another? Can we restore the power of the **individual** so that all the people are clearly united for **liberty, freedom** and **happiness**?

Note: Know that this is at our core and cannot be defeated. It is this that is our real strength, our real power and is our greatest defense as well as our greatest offense.

Read the following pages with an open mind. Do not judge! Just allow the information to settle in you where it chooses. You will soon realize that you are important and have the power to do something. You will realize, you are not just dreaming....**You are the dream.**

SIMPLICITY

It is really simple…it's about "YOU". I am…you are! The individual is the core. So how do I help you to understand this and still keep it simple?

Life is a gift. I am, as you are, a gift to life.

Only through simplicity can we truly connect with each other and with all of life.

Only through simplicity can our natural birthright be truly free.

Only as simplicity will beauty, peace, joy and love be free.

Only as simplicity can we truly "Dare to Be".

INTRODUCTION

"When hope changes to knowing, consciousness changes or transforms from dreaming to being the dream."

This book and its simplicity opens the door for each one of us to once again understand what democracy really means and what the intent of our forefathers really was. Our system is unique because, unlike other systems, it centers around the people. The **individual is the core** and is never to be expensed out by a group. Of the people....for the people...and by the people; not of the group....for the group...and by the group.

Groups or factions always represent a minority, not the majority and serve their own interests. In these circumstances the "American Dream" cannot survive, opening the door to despotism.

You are the dream and always have been. Society and our way of life can change. It's up to us, each and every one of us is important and together, in common purpose, honoring liberty and freedom, we can do anything we set our focus on. No one group can stand in our way.

The simple insights expressed in this book will change your consciousness and open your world. You will know a power, a different power, you didn't know you had or even existed. You will feel a peace that you have never experienced. You will see beauty continuously unfolding before your very own eyes. You will be a new found joy. Life is truly a gift…you are a gift to life. You deserve this and much more.

Civil society and democracy is not just a system of governance; it is a way of life, a consciousness, and the rewards are…endless.

THE SEVEN SEEDS OF AMERICAN DEMOCRACY

The following seven seeds are the core of a true democracy and of central focus in this book:

- REALIZE YOUR OWN IMPORTANCE

- GET INVOLVED

- DEMAND INFORMATION

- VOTE

- ELECT LEADERS

- SET PRIORITIES AND DEFINE THE ISSUES

- HOLD THEM ACCOUNTABLE FOR THEIR ACTIONS AND RESPONSIBLE FOR THE RESULTS.

These are expanded on in Section III.

SECTION I

THE "AMERICAN DREAM"

THE "AMERICAN DREAM"

*CIVIL SOCIETY: A social organization in which the **individual** is important and has a full voice in his/her direction, under a system where the value of each **individual** is united in **common cause**: 'Life is a gift for all individuals, and all individuals are a gift to life.'*

With this at our core, oppression disappears and has no chance of returning.

A civil society is a strong society, where our interests -- economic, religious, social and political -- are balanced for the benefit of all. Our best defense is a debt free country with a powerful military (non-aggressive…a deterrent only), and a harmonious society where individuals are free to grow and express themselves as they honor each other's individual **freedom** and **liberty**. This is also our best offense.

It is a society based on the premise "of the people … for the people … and by the people," and a system of majority rule equally representing each individual and not at the expense of the other. In other words; everyone benefits -- even if they were outvoted. This way, no group may gain control at the expense of others.

Our forefathers were very clear as to the problems inherent in party (group) systems, which actually function under minority rule, and thus open the door to despotism: "of the group… for the group… and by the group."

When this happens, the **individual** no longer matters. His/her **individual freedom** and **liberty** disappears, as the group dictates what is to be done.

In short, "civil society" represents harmony among its individuals, promoting a sort of equality where it is both easy and encouraged for the individual to participate in its affairs. It features a government based on democracy that guarantees freedom of action and speech for all its people, in all areas -- including the religious, social, political and economic phases of societal life." Individuals united in **common cause** eliminate the power and danger of group rule and its despotic tendency.

So when did civil society and democracy begin in this country?

During the early 1600s, people started migrating, mostly from England, to America. They sought a new promised land, uncharted and unknown, but a place to start a new dream, an "American Dream."

It was certainly a dangerous trip, where many would not survive the journey and many more would not survive the ruggedness and obstacles of their new land. So we must wonder at first, why were they so willing to risk their lives for hard work and a great struggle against heavy odds?

The answer is simple: Although there were some who came for the adventure or expecting to strike it rich, most people came to flee some sort of oppression. Their lives in Europe had been a struggle that saw no hope.

Whether the oppression had been religious, political, economic or social, they had had enough ... enough ... enough! They were willing to risk it all for the ultimate, for a chance at **liberty** and **freedom**. Their credo, prefiguring one of their later followers, was: 'Give me liberty, I'll chance death ... it's worth it.' [See Patrick Henry speech, pp. 17]

And so the seeds were planted. Many people -- of many different backgrounds, beliefs and ways of life -- landed in a new promised land, fertilizing our soil with their own richness. They had to unite in **common cause** to survive, and thus American democracy and its civil society was born.

They worked hard and the country grew, as more and more people came to fulfill their dreams. As they did, they also began to attract the attention of the rulers back home, as this new country and its riches became more attractive to the English rule. Greed, power and its control began to rule. All too soon, the honeymoon was over.

Oppression began slowly, but grew rapidly until the people could take no more. They soon found themselves right back where their ancestors had started in Europe, living in a prison, with the same oppressors they thought they had escaped.

Let's be clear here: We were the citizens of English Colonies under an English government, and thus entitled to the English free system of laws. However, under George III our freedoms were being rapidly eroded and transforming into a condition of 'Despotic Slavery.' For years we addressed each of these issues, both on our own soil and at the foot of the throne in Mother England. But it was all to no avail, leaving us with no room for hope.

The oppression increased, as our trade was cut off, more taxes were imposed, and British troops and navies were vastly increased. At the same time, the English free system of laws were slowly being removed, as were most of our own valuable laws. Our form of government was being changed, and legislatures were even being suspended.

Meanwhile, the British troops were being allowed a broad freedom of violence to be practiced on innocent citizens. Soon they had invested in themselves the sole right to legislate as they pleased. 'Despotism' had taken over and we were 'Despotic Slaves'. Enough…Enough …Enough!

On July 4th, 1776, the final draft of the 'Declaration Of Independence' was finished:

> *"We hold these truths to be self-evident, that all men are created equal, that they are endowed by their Creator with certain unalienable Rights, that among these are Life, Lib-*

*erty, and the pursuit of Happiness. ... That to
secure these rights, Governments are instituted among Men, deriving their just powers
from the consent of the governed, ... That
whenever any Form of Government becomes
destructive of these ends it is the Right of the
People to alter or abolish it, and to institute
new Government, laying its foundation on
such principals and organizing its powers in
such form as to them shall seem most likely to
effect their Safety and Happiness."* [see pp. 22
for full text]

Independence was declared, with the passion of the
people as its power. Patrick Henry restated the premise
with a bit more eloquence, "but as for me, give me liberty
or give me death!" [see pp. 17]

United in **common cause**, with a power not to be
destroyed, **freedom** and **liberty** were preserved. After a
bitter struggle, the war was won. We were free and our
rights restored.

Now what were we to do? How were we to protect
these rights? As thirteen individual states or one United
States? The process began. A new system of government
had to be installed, not just laws, but a way of life, a consciousness -- the same consciousness that had united in
common cause against England and was proven inde-
structible must now be allowed to grow, to decide and
preserve its own destiny.

In 1781, The Articles of Confederation [see pp. 30] were ratified. This was a start in uniting thirteen now independent states. However, there were still major problems, including no way to raise funds for common purposes or to standardize laws.

We now had thirteen individual ways of doing things, with no strong central government to unify them. The unit that had broken away from England was now divided, with no standardized way of protecting the individual in commercial, political or social areas of their lives; nor was there common protection against foreign influence. The doors were wide open for power-hungry people, at home or abroad, to take advantage of the freedom of the individual. Would we once again be open prey? No, said many of the newly made Americans!

We were loosely joined, and yet we recognized the importance of strengthening our union. A convention was called to revise the 'Articles Of Confederation' and create one nation of thirteen equally represented states. On September 17, 1787, the final draft of the Constitution [see pp. 35] was signed by thirty-nine of the forty-two delegates, and sent to the states for ratification. On March 4, 1789, the first Congress met and on April 30, George Washington was inaugurated our first President.

Unity at last. American democracy was officially born. The people had spoken and the **common cause** of the **individual** was the focus of their intentions.

Although many disagreements and heated debates now ensued, the people did not lose their focus on what was really important, in the temptations of personal gain. We came together, in one of the early examples of civil society in action. [Note: the actual Constitution will be discussed later in Section II.]

What was the consciousness of our forefathers, and what were their concerns? What was this idea of "democracy" all about to them … in its real intent?

George Washington was very clear on this and openly expressed so in both his 'First Inaugural Address' [see pp. 75] and his 'Farewell Address' [see pp. 81]; Thomas Jefferson echoed these beliefs in his own 'First Inaugural Address'.[see pp. 107] (Note: These are just a few examples. Many more can be found in the various papers of all of our Founding Fathers, reflecting the same sentiments.) In each case, the core intent was the same, and important to all of them. This would not be a mere Government, but a consciousness … a way of life.

George Washington clearly showed his humility in his 'First Inaugural Address' as he referred to the 'Spirit of the People' as an embodiment of "the Almighty Being with an invisible hand. A Spirit that rules the universe and connects as well as flows through us all."

It's this 'Spirit' deeply embedded in all of us that gave us the power to unite in **Common Cause** and overcome unbeatable odds to protect our liberty and freedom. This was also at the core of our new government. The individual was important, and each individual's liberty and happiness must be sacred and protected. A government of the masses, based on the individual, was vastly different from other forms of society.

Later on in this address, he states;

> *"In these honorable qualifications I behold the surest pledges that as on one side no local prejudices or attachments, no separate views nor party animosities, will misdirect the comprehensive and equal eye which ought to watch over this great assemblage of communities and interests, so, on another, that the foundation of our national policy will be laid in the pure and immutable principles of private morality, and the preeminence of free government be exemplified by all the attributes which can win the affections of its citizens and command respect of the world. I dwell on this prospect with every satisfaction which an ardent love for my country can inspire, since there is no truth more thoroughly established than that there exists in the economy and course of nature an indissoluble union between virtue and happiness; between duty and advantage; between the genuine maxims of an honest and magnanimous policy and the solid rewards of public prosperity and felicity...[see pp. 78].*

As you can see from George Washington's own words, democracy, this new form of government, was not just a government but a consciousness or a way of life. This spirit of democracy is what makes it work. Liberty and Happiness, for each and every citizen equally, were important to its citizens. The government was not only to govern the people but to be **administrated** and **overseen** by the people.

Now let's move on. George Washington's intention was to retire after his first term, and in May 1792, he sent James Madison an outline of the points he wanted to cover in his Farewell Address, asking him to write an address for him. Later, when he decided to take a second term, he tabled this idea.

In 1796, at the end of his second term, he sent the draft to Alexander Hamilton for input and revising. With further consultation from John Jay, the final address was finished. Although the address was never verbally given, it was published in Philadelphia in the 'American Daily Advertiser' on September 19, 1796. Later, it appeared in newspapers all over the country.

Washington discussed the many debates involved in forming the Constitution, as well as certain dangers that needed close attention: the perils of party or group influence, involvement in foreign affairs, a too powerful military, and the accumulation of debt, to name just a few of his targets. Meanwhile, he continually interweaved references to unity, freedom, liberty, and the happiness of every citizen, into his text. As he put it: "In this sense it is, that your union ought to be considered as a main prop of your liberty. And that the love of the one ought to endear you to the perseveration of the other."

He spent a great deal of time talking about the dangers of party (groups or factions) influence on individual liberty. Any organized faction, such as a party, is a minority; although they may appear to have the interests of the nation (all of its citizens) in mind, it is ultimately the will of the party that takes priority: ":.. they are likely in the course of time and things, to become potent engines, by which cunning, ambitious and unprincipled men will be enabled to subvert the Power of People, the very engines which have lifted them to unjust dominion."

He goes on to declare that this spirit of party is rooted in the strongest passions of the human mind: "… sooner or later the chief of some prevailing faction more able or more fortunate than his competitors, turns this disposition to the purposes of his own elevation, on the ruins of Public Liberty." This trend, he notes, leads to despotism.

He goes on to emphasize the necessity of staying neutral and not getting involved in the affairs of other nations. Foreign influence or the involvement in foreign affairs makes us a slave to their cause, creates animosity with other nations, and compromises/diverts the interests of our own nation and its citizens.

Every time you promote conflict, he warns, peace is eroded: "The Great Rule of conduct for us, in regard to foreign Nations is in extending our commercial relations to have with them as little political connection as possible," (For example, Europe's primary interests are different than ours, having little or no relation to us. In turning our attention to their interests, we turn away from our very own, jeopardizing our own peace, prosperity, freedom and safety.)

Another thing Washington stressed in that piece is the need for a nation to be debt free. A strong nation must be very conscious of keeping its economic state in good order. Finally it is clear that he recognized the need to be very diligent for the growth and preservation of democracy, to promote a Government of the people, for the people, and by the people, with each and every person taking a role. It was a way of life, a consciousness, in place to preserve liberty and happiness for all. All we can say is, Thanks George!

Now let's say hello to Tom: Thomas Jefferson, another one of our forefathers, who was influential in both the Declaration of Independence and the Constitution, served as Secretary of State under George Washington, Vice President under John Adams and was then our third President for two terms. Another humble servant of common efforts and common good. "All, too, will bear in mind this sacred principle, that through the will of the majority, is in all cases to prevail, that will to be rightful must be reasonable, that the minority possess their equal rights, which equal law must protect, and to violate would be **oppression**." [see pp. 107] [Note: Once again, we must remember that oppression was the main reason people migrated to this country, as well as the reason we revolted. It must always be guarded against.]

Jefferson re-emphasized the importance of unity, happiness and the strength of the individual in all phases of life: "Equal and exact justice to all men, of whatever state or persuasion, religious or political; peace, commerce and honest friendship with all nations, entangling alliances with none; ... a jealous care of the right of election by the people, ... absolute acquiescence in the discussions of the majority."

He spoke of the importance of our various freedoms, the preservation of the public faith, unity along our road to peace, liberty and safety. He ended by referring to the **Spirit** which unites and flows through us all: "and may that Infinite Power which rules the destinies of the universe lead our councils to what is best, and give them a favorable issue for your peace and prosperity."

This is what democracy and its way of life meant to our forefathers. Unfortunately, over time, due in part to technical advances and population growth, we have strayed from their intended path.

[Examples and some key points will be covered later in Section II.]

GREAT DOCUMENTS OF

AMERICAN HISTORY

The following are considered the great documents of American history:

- Patrick Henry Speech, March 23, 1775

- The Declaration of Independence

- Articles of Confederation

- The Constitution of the United States

- The Bill of Rights (and other amendments)

- George Washington: 1st Inaugural Address, 1789

- George Washington: Farewell Address, 1796

- Thomas Jefferson: 1st Inaugural Address, 1801

They have been included in this section so that you may have a chance to read them in their entirety; after all, they are central to our definition of a democracy.

PATRICK HENRY SPEECH, MARCH 23, 1775

Following the Boston Tea Party, Dec. 16, 1773, in which American Colonists dumped 342 containers of tea into the Boston harbor, the British Parliament enacted a series of Acts in response to the rebellion in Massachusetts. In May of 1774, General Thomas Gage, commander of all British military forces in the colonies, arrived in Boston, followed by the arrival of four regiments of British troops. The First Continental Congress met in the fall of 1774 in Philadelphia with 56 American delegates, representing every colony, except Georgia. On September 17, the Congress declared its opposition to the repressive Acts of Parliament, saying they are "not to be obeyed," and also promoted the formation of local militia units. Thus economic and military tensions between the colonists and the British escalated. In February of 1775, a provincial congress was held in Massachusetts during which John Hancock and Joseph Warren began defensive preparations for a state of war. The English Parliament then declared Massachusetts to be in a state of rebellion.

On March 23, in Virginia, the largest colony in America, a meeting of the colony's delegates was held in St. John's church in Richmond. Resolutions were presented by Patrick Henry putting the colony of Virginia "into a posture of defense...embodying, arming, and disciplining such a number of men as may be sufficient for that purpose." Before the vote was taken on his resolutions, Henry delivered the speech below, imploring the delegates to vote in favor. He spoke without any notes in a voice that became louder and louder, climaxing with the now famous ending. Following his speech, the vote was taken in which his resolutions passed by a narrow margin, and thus Virginia joined in the American Revolution.

No man thinks more highly than I do of the patriotism, as well as abilities, of the very worthy gentlemen who have just addressed the House. But different men often see the same subject in different lights; and, therefore, I hope that it will not be thought disrespectful to those gentlemen, if, entertaining as I do opinions of a character very opposite to theirs, I shall speak forth my sentiments freely and without reserve.

This is no time for ceremony. The question before the House is one of awful moment to this country. For my own part I consider it as nothing less than a question of freedom or slavery; and in proportion to the magnitude of the subject ought to be the freedom of the debate. It is only in this way that we can hope to arrive at truth, and fulfill the great responsibility which we hold to God and our country. Should I keep back my opinions at such a time, through fear of giving offense, I should consider myself as guilty of treason towards my country, and of an act of disloyalty towards the majesty of heaven, which I revere above all earthly kings.

Mr. President, it is natural to man to indulge in the illusions of hope. We are apt to shut our eyes against a painful truth, and listen to the song of that siren, till she transforms us into beasts. Is this the part of wise men, engaged in a great and arduous struggle for liberty? Are we disposed to be of the number of those who, having eyes, see not, and having ears, hear not, the things which so nearly concern their temporal salvation?

For my part, whatever anguish of spirit it may cost, I am willing to know the whole truth -- to know the worst and to provide for it. I have but one lamp by which my feet are guided; and that is the lamp of experience. I know of no way of judging of the future but by the past. And judging by the past, I wish to know what there has been in the conduct of the British ministry for the last ten years, to justify those hopes with which gentlemen have been pleased to solace themselves and the House?

Is it that insidious smile with which our petition has been lately received? Trust it not, sir; it will prove a snare to your feet. Suffer not yourselves to be betrayed with a kiss. Ask yourselves how this gracious reception of our petition comports with these warlike preparations which cover our waters and darken our land. Are fleets and armies necessary to a work of love and reconciliation? Have we shown ourselves so unwilling to be reconciled that force must be called in to win back our love? Let us not deceive ourselves, sir. These are the implements of war and subjugation -- the last arguments to which kings resort. I ask gentlemen, sir, what means this martial array, if its purpose be not to force us to submission? Can gentlemen assign any other possible motives for it? Has Great Britain any enemy, in this quarter of the world, to call for all this accumulation of navies and armies?

No, sir, she has none. They are meant for us; they can be meant for no other. They are sent over to bind and rivet upon us those chains which the British ministry have been so long forging. And what have we to oppose to them? Shall we try argument? Sir, we have been trying that for the last ten years. Have we anything new to offer on the subject? Nothing.

We have held the subject up in every light of which it is capable; but it has been all in vain. Shall we resort to entreaty and humble supplication? What terms shall we find which have not been already exhausted? Let us not, I beseech you, sir, deceive ourselves longer.

Sir, we have done everything that could be done to avert the storm which is now coming on. We have petitioned; we have remonstrated; we have supplicated; we have prostrated ourselves before the throne, and have implored its interposition to arrest the tyrannical hands of the ministry and Parliament.

Our petitions have been slighted; our remonstrances have produced additional violence and insult; our supplications have been disregarded; and we have been spurned, with contempt, from the foot of the throne. In vain, after these things, may we indulge the fond hope of peace and reconciliation. There is no longer any room for hope.

If we wish to be free -- if we mean to preserve inviolate those inestimable privileges for which we have been so long contending -- if we mean not basely to abandon the noble struggle in which we have been so long engaged, and which we have pledged ourselves never to abandon until the glorious object of our contest shall be obtained, we must fight! I repeat it, sir, we must fight! An appeal to arms and to the God of Hosts is all that is left us!

They tell us, sir, that we are weak -- unable to cope with so formidable an adversary. But when shall we be stronger? Will it be the next week, or the next year? Will it be when we are totally disarmed, and when a British guard shall be stationed in every house? Shall we gather strength by irresolution and inaction? Shall we acquire the means of effectual resistance, by lying supinely on our backs, and hugging the delusive phantom of hope, until our enemies shall have bound us hand and foot?

Sir, we are not weak, if we make a proper use of the means which the God of nature hath placed in our power. Three millions of people, armed in the holy cause of liberty, and in such a country as that which we possess, are invincible by any force which our enemy can send against us. Besides, sir, we shall not fight our battles alone. There is a just God who presides over the destinies of nations, and who will raise up friends to fight our battles for us.

The battle, sir, is not to the strong alone; it is to the vigilant, the active, the brave. Besides, sir, we have no election. If we were base enough to desire it, it is now too late to retire from the contest. There is no retreat but in submission and slavery! Our chains are forged! Their clanking may be heard on the plains of Boston! The war is inevitable -- and let it come! I repeat it, sir, let it come!

It is in vain, sir, to extenuate the matter. Gentlemen may cry, "Peace! Peace!" -- but there is no peace. The war is actually begun! The next gale that sweeps from the north will bring to our ears the clash of resounding arms! Our brethren are already in the field! Why stand we here idle? What is it that gentlemen wish? What would they have? Is life so dear, or peace so sweet, as to be purchased at the price of chains and slavery? Forbid it, Almighty God! I know not what course others may take; but as for me, give me liberty, or give me death!

Patrick Henry - March 23, 1775

THE DECLARATION OF INDEPENDENCE

IN CONGRESS, July 4, 1776.

The unanimous Declaration of the thirteen united States of America,

When in the Course of human events, it becomes necessary for one people to dissolve the political bands which have connected them with another, and to assume among the powers of the earth, the separate and equal station to which the Laws of Nature and of Nature's God entitle them, a decent respect to the opinions of mankind requires that they should declare the causes which impel them to the separation.

We hold these truths to be self-evident, that all men are created equal, that they are endowed by their Creator with certain unalienable Rights, that among these are Life, Liberty and the pursuit of Happiness.--That to secure these rights, Governments are instituted among Men, deriving their just powers from the consent of the governed, --That whenever any Form of Government becomes destructive of these ends, it is the Right of the People to alter or to abolish it, and to institute new Government, laying its foundation on such principles and organizing its powers in such form, as to them shall seem most likely to effect their Safety and Happiness. Prudence, indeed, will dictate that Governments long established should not be changed for light and transient causes; and accordingly all experience hath shewn, that mankind are more disposed to suffer, while evils are sufferable, than to right themselves by abolishing the forms to which they are accustomed. But when a long train of abuses and usurpations, pursuing invariably the same Object evinces a design to reduce them under absolute Despotism, it is their right, it is their duty, to throw off such Government, and to provide new Guards for their future security.--Such has been the patient sufferance of these Colonies; and such is now the necessity which constrains them to alter their former Systems of Government. The history of the present King of Great Britain is a history of repeated injuries and usurpations, all having in direct object the establishment of an absolute Tyranny over these States. To prove this, let Facts be submitted to a candid world.

He has refused his Assent to Laws, the most wholesome and necessary for the public good.

He has forbidden his Governors to pass Laws of immediate and pressing importance, unless suspended in their operation till his Assent should be obtained; and when so suspended, he has utterly neglected to attend to them.

He has refused to pass other Laws for the accommodation of large districts of people, unless those people would relinquish the right of Representation in the Legislature, a right inestimable to them and formidable to tyrants only.

He has called together legislative bodies at places unusual, uncomfortable, and distant from the depository of their public Records, for the sole purpose of fatiguing them into compliance with his measures.

He has dissolved Representative Houses repeatedly, for opposing with manly firmness his invasions on the rights of the people.

He has refused for a long time, after such dissolutions, to cause others to be elected; whereby the Legislative powers, incapable of Annihilation, have returned to the People at large for their exercise; the State remaining in the mean time exposed to all the dangers of invasion from without, and convulsions within.

He has endeavoured to prevent the population of these States; for that purpose obstructing the Laws for Naturalization of Foreigners; refusing to pass others to encourage their migrations hither, and raising the conditions of new Appropriations of Lands.

He has obstructed the Administration of Justice, by refusing his Assent to Laws for establishing Judiciary powers.

He has made Judges dependent on his Will alone, for the tenure of their offices, and the amount and payment of their salaries.

He has erected a multitude of New Offices, and sent hither swarms of Officers to harass our people, and eat out their substance.

He has kept among us, in times of peace, Standing Armies without the Consent of our legislatures.

He has affected to render the Military independent of and superior to the Civil power.

He has combined with others to subject us to a jurisdiction foreign to our constitution, and unacknowledged by our laws; giving his Assent to their Acts of pretended Legislation:

For Quartering large bodies of armed troops among us:

For protecting them, by a mock Trial, from punishment for any Murders which they should commit on the Inhabitants of these States:

For cutting off our Trade with all parts of the world:

For imposing Taxes on us without our Consent:

For depriving us in many cases, of the benefits of Trial by Jury:

For transporting us beyond Seas to be tried for pretended offences

For abolishing the free System of English Laws in a neighbouring Province, establishing therein an Arbitrary government, and enlarging its Boundaries so as to render it at once an example and fit instrument for introducing the same absolute rule into these Colonies:

For taking away our Charters, abolishing our most valuable Laws, and altering fundamentally the Forms of our Governments:

For suspending our own Legislatures, and declaring themselves invested with power to legislate for us in all cases whatsoever.

He has abdicated Government here, by declaring us out of his Protection and waging War against us.

He has plundered our seas, ravaged our Coasts, burnt our towns, and destroyed the lives of our people.

He is at this time transporting large Armies of foreign Mercenaries to compleat the works of death, desolation and tyranny, already begun with circumstances of Cruelty & perfidy scarcely paralleled in the most barbarous ages, and totally unworthy the Head of a civilized nation.

He has constrained our fellow Citizens taken Captive on the high Seas to bear Arms against their Country, to become the executioners of their friends and Brethren, or to fall themselves by their Hands.

He has excited domestic insurrections amongst us, and has endeavoured to bring on the inhabitants of our frontiers, the merciless Indian Savages, whose known rule of warfare, is an undistinguished destruction of all ages, sexes and conditions.

In every stage of these Oppressions We have Petitioned for Redress in the most humble terms: Our repeated Petitions have been answered only by repeated injury. A Prince whose character is thus marked by every act which may define a Tyrant, is unfit to be the ruler of a free people.

Nor have We been wanting in attentions to our Brittish brethren. We have warned them from time to time of attempts by their legislature to extend an unwarrantable jurisdiction over us. We have reminded them of the circumstances of our emigration and settlement here. We have appealed to their native justice and magnanimity, and we have conjured them by the ties of our common kindred to disavow these usurpations, which, would inevitably interrupt our connections and correspondence. They too have been deaf to the voice of justice and of consanguinity. We must, therefore, acquiesce in the necessity, which denounces our Separation, and hold them, as we hold the rest of mankind, Enemies in War, in Peace Friends.

We, therefore, the Representatives of the united States of America, in General Congress, Assembled, appealing to the Supreme Judge of the world for the rectitude of our intentions, do, in the Name, and by Authority of the good People of these Colonies, solemnly publish and declare, That these United Colonies are, and of Right ought to be Free and Independent States; that they are Absolved from all Allegiance to the British Crown, and that all political connection between them and the State of Great Britain, is and ought to be totally dissolved; and that as Free and Independent States, they have full Power to levy War, conclude Peace, contract Alliances, establish Commerce, and to do all other Acts and Things which Independent States may of right do. And for the support of this Declaration, with a firm reliance on the protection of divine Providence, we mutually pledge to each other our Lives, our Fortunes and our sacred Honor.

Georgia: Button Gwinnett, Lyman Hall, George Walton

North Carolina: William Hooper, Joseph Hewes, John Penn

South Carolina: Edward Rutledge, Thomas Heyward, Jr., Thomas Lynch, Jr., Arthur Middleton

Maryland: Samuel Chase, William Paca, Thomas Stone, Charles Carroll of Carrollton

Virginia: George Wythe, Richard Henry Lee, Thomas Jefferson, Benjamin Harrison, Thomas Nelson, Jr., Francis Lightfoot Lee, Carter Braxton

Pennsylvania: Robert Morris, Benjamin Rush, Benjamin Franklin, John Morton, George *Clymer, James Smith, George Taylor, James Wilson, George Ross*

Delaware: Caesar Rodney, George Read, Thomas McKean

New York: William Floyd, Philip Livingston, Francis Lewis, Lewis Morris

New Jersey: Richard Stockton, John Witherspoon, Francis Hopkinson, John Hart. Abraham Clark

New Hampshire: Josiah Bartlett, William Whipple

Massachusetts: John Hancock, Samuel Adams, John Adams, Robert Treat Paine, Elbridge Gerry

Rhode Island: Stephen Hopkins, William Ellery

Connecticut: Roger Sherman. Samuel Huntington. William Williams. Oliver Wolcott

New Hampshire: Matthew Thornton

ARTICLES OF CONFEDERATION

Articles of Confederation and perpetual Union, entered into proposed by the Delegates of the several Colonies of New Hampshire, in general Congress met at Philadelphia, May 10, 1775.

Article I. The Name of this Confederacy shall henceforth be The United Colonies of North America.

Article II. The said United Colonies hereby severally enter into a firm League of Friendship with each other, binding on themselves and their Posterity, for their common Defense, against their Enemies for the Security of their Liberties and Properties, the Safety of their Persons and Families, and their mutual and general Welfare.

Article III. That each Colony shall enjoy and retain as much as it may think fit of its own present Laws, Customs, Rights, Privileges, and peculiar Jurisdictions within its own Limits; and may amend its own Constitution as shall seem best to its own Assembly or Convention.

Article IV. That for the more convenient Management of general Interests, Delegates shall be annually elected in each Colony to meet in General Congress at such Time and Place as shall be agreed on in the next preceding Congress. Only where particular Circumstances do not make a Deviation necessary, it is understood to be a Rule, that each succeeding Congress be held in a different Colony till the whole Number be gone through, and so in perpetual Rotation; and that accordingly the next Congress after the present shall be held at Annapolis in Maryland.

Article V. That the Power and Duty of the Congress shall extend to the Determining on War and Peace, to sending and receiving ambassadors, and entering into Alliances, the Reconciliation with Great Britain, the Settling all Disputes and Differences between Colony and Colony about Limits or any other cause if such should arise; and the Planting of new Colonies when proper. The Congress shall also make such general Ordinances as thought necessary to the General Welfare, particular Assemblies cannot be competent to; viz. those that may relate to our general Commerce; or general Currency; to the Establishment of Posts; and the Regulation of our common Forces. The Congress shall also have the Appointment of all General Officers, civil and military, appertaining to the general Confederacy, such as General Treasurer, Secretary.

Article VI. All Charges of Wars, and all other general Expenses to be incurred for the common Welfare, shall be defrayed out of a common Treasury, which is to be supplied by each Colony in proportion to its Number of Male Polls between 16 and 60 Years of Age; the Taxes for paying that proportion are to be laid and levied by the Laws of each Colony.

Article VII. The Number of Delegates to be elected and sent to the Congress by each Colony, shall be regulated from time to time by the Number of such Polls returned; so as that one Delegate be allowed for every 5000 Polls. And the Delegates are to bring with them to every Congress, an authenticated Return of the number of Polls in the respective Provinces which is to be annually triennially taken for the Purposes above mentioned.

Article VIII. At every Meeting of the Congress One half of the Members returned exclusive of Proxies be necessary to make a Quorum, and Each Delegate at the Congress, shall have a Vote in all Cases; and if necessarily absent, shall be allowed to appoint any other Delegate from the same Colony to be his Proxy, who may vote for him.

Article IX. An executive Council shall be appointed by the Congress out of their own Body, consisting of 12 Persons; of whom in the first Appointment one Third, viz. 4, shall be for one year, 4 for two Years, and 4 for three Years; and as the said Terms expire, the Vacancy shall be filled by Appointments for three Years, whereby One Third of the Members will be changed annually. And each Person who has served the said Term of three Years as Counselor, shall have a Respite of three Years, before he can be elected again. This Council (of whom two thirds shall be a Quorum), in the Recess of the Congress is to execute what shall have been enjoined thereby; to manage the general continental Business and Interests to receive Applications from foreign Countries; to prepare Matters for the Consideration of the Congress; to fill up Pro tempore general continental Offices that fall vacant; and to draw on the General Treasurer for such Monies as may be necessary for general Services, & appropriated by the Congress to such Services.

Article X. No Colony shall engage in an offensive War with any Nation of Indians without the Consent of the Congress, or great Council above mentioned, who are first to consider the Justice and Necessity of such War.

Article XI. A perpetual Alliance offensive and defensive, is to be entered into as soon as may be with the Six Nations; their Limits to be ascertained and secured to them; their Land not to be encroached on, nor any private or Colony Purchases made of them hereafter to be held good; nor any Contract for Lands to be made but between the Great Council of the Indians at Onondaga and the General Congress. The Boundaries and Lands of all the other Indians shall also be ascertained and secured to them in the same manner; and Persons appointed to reside among them in proper Districts, who shall take care to prevent Injustice in the Trade with them, and be enabled at our general Expense by occasional small Supplies, to relieve their personal Wants and Distresses. And all Purchases from them shall be by the Congress for the General Advantage and Benefit of the United Colonies.

Article XII. As all new Institutions may have Imperfections which only Time and Experience can discover, it is agreed, That the General Congress from time to time shall propose such Amendments of this Constitution as may be found necessary; which being approved by a Majority of the Colony Assemblies, shall be equally binding with the rest of the Articles of this Confederation.

Article XIII. Any and every Colony from Great Britain upon the Continent of North America and not at present engaged in our Association may upon Application and joining the said Association be received into this Confederation, viz. Ireland, the West India Islands, Quebec, St. Johns, Nova Scotia, Bermudas, and the East and West Floridas; and shall thereupon be entitled to all the Advantages of our Union, mutual Assistance and Commerce.

These Articles shall be proposed to the several Provincial Conventions or Assemblies, to be by them considered, and if approved they are advised to empower their Delegates to agree to and ratify the same in the ensuing Congress. After which the Union thereby established is to continue firm till the Terms of Reconciliation proposed in the Petition of the last Congress to the King are agreed to; till the Acts since made restraining the American Commerce and Fisheries are repealed; till Reparation is made for the Injury done to Boston by shutting up its Port; for the Burning of Charlestown; and for the Expense of this unjust War; and till all the British Troops are withdrawn from America. On the Arrival of these Events the Colonies shall return to their former Connection and Friendship with Britain: But on Failure thereof this Confederation is to be perpetual.

THE CONSTITUTION OF THE UNITED STATES

Preamble: We the People of the United States, in Order to form a more perfect Union, establish Justice, insure domestic Tranquility, provide for the common defence, promote the general Welfare, and secure the Blessings of Liberty to ourselves and our Posterity, do ordain and establish this Constitution for the United States of America.

ARTICLE. I. - THE LEGISLATIVE BRANCH

Section 1 - The Legislature

All legislative Powers herein granted shall be vested in a Congress of the United States, which shall consist of a Senate and House of Representatives.

Section 2 - The House

The House of Representatives shall be composed of Members chosen every second Year by the People of the several States, and the Electors in each State shall have the Qualifications requisite for Electors of the most numerous Branch of the State Legislature.

No Person shall be a Representative who shall not have attained to the Age of twenty five Years, and been seven Years a Citizen of the United States, and who shall not, when elected, be an Inhabitant of that State in which he shall be chosen.

(Representatives and direct Taxes shall be apportioned among the several States which may be included within this Union, according to their respective Numbers, which shall be determined by adding to the whole Number of free Persons, including those bound to Service for a Term of Years, and excluding Indians not taxed, three fifths of all other Persons.) (The previous sentence in parentheses was modified by the 14th Amendment, section 2.) The actual Enumeration shall be made within three Years after the first Meeting of the Congress of the United States, and within every subsequent Term of ten Years, in such Manner as they shall by Law direct. The Number of Representatives shall not exceed one for every thirty Thousand, but each State shall have at Least one Representative; and until such enumeration shall be made, the State of New Hampshire shall be entitled to chuse three, Massachusetts eight, Rhode Island and Providence Plantations one, Connecticut five, New York six, New Jersey four, Pennsylvania eight, Delaware one, Maryland six, Virginia ten, North Carolina five, South Carolina five and Georgia three.

When vacancies happen in the Representation from any State, the Executive Authority thereof shall issue Writs of Election to fill such Vacancies.

The House of Representatives shall chuse their Speaker and other Officers; and shall have the sole Power of Impeachment.

Section 3 - The Senate

The Senate of the United States shall be composed of two Senators from each State, (chosen by the Legislature thereof,) (The preceding words in parentheses superseded by 17th Amendment, section 1.) for six Years; and each Senator shall have one Vote.

Immediately after they shall be assembled in Consequence of the first Election, they shall be divided as equally as may be into three Classes. The Seats of the Senators of the first Class shall be vacated at the Expiration of the second Year, of the second Class at the Expiration of the fourth Year, and of the third Class at the Expiration of the sixth Year, so that one third may be chosen every second Year; (and if Vacancies happen by Resignation, or otherwise, during the Recess of the Legislature of any State, the Executive thereof may make temporary Appointments until the next Meeting of the Legislature, which shall then fill such Vacancies.) (The preceding words in parentheses were superseded by the 17th Amendment, section 2.)

No person shall be a Senator who shall not have attained to the Age of thirty Years, and been nine Years a Citizen of the United States, and who shall not, when elected, be an Inhabitant of that State for which he shall be chosen.

The Vice President of the United States shall be President of the Senate, but shall have no Vote, unless they be equally divided.

The Senate shall chuse their other Officers, and also a President pro tempore, in the absence of the Vice President, or when he shall exercise the Office of President of the United States.

The Senate shall have the sole Power to try all Impeachments. When sitting for that Purpose, they shall be on Oath or Affirmation. When the President of the United States is tried, the Chief Justice shall preside: And no Person shall be convicted without the Concurrence of two thirds of the Members present.

Judgment in Cases of Impeachment shall not extend further than to removal from Office, and disqualification to hold and enjoy any Office of honor, Trust or Profit under the United States: but the Party convicted shall nevertheless be liable and subject to Indictment, Trial, Judgment and Punishment, according to Law.

Section 4 - Elections, Meetings

The Times, Places and Manner of holding Elections for Senators and Representatives, shall be prescribed in each State by the Legislature thereof; but the Congress may at any time by Law make or alter such Regulations, except as to the Place of Chusing Senators.

The Congress shall assemble at least once in every Year, and such Meeting shall (be on the first Monday in December,) (The preceding words in parentheses were superseded by the 20th Amendment, section 2.) unless they shall by Law appoint a different Day.

Section 5 - Membership, Rules, Journals, Adjournment

Each House shall be the Judge of the Elections, Returns and Qualifications of its own Members, and a Majority of each shall constitute a Quorum to do Business; but a smaller number may adjourn from day to day, and may be authorized to compel the Attendance of absent Members, in such Manner, and under such Penalties as each House may provide.

Each House may determine the Rules of its Proceedings, punish its Members for disorderly Behavior, and, with the Concurrence of two-thirds, expel a Member.

Each House shall keep a Journal of its Proceedings, and from time to time publish the same, excepting such Parts as may in their Judgment require Secrecy; and the Yeas and Nays of the Members of either House on any question shall, at the Desire of one fifth of those Present, be entered on the Journal.

Neither House, during the Session of Congress, shall, without the Consent of the other, adjourn for more than three days, nor to any other Place than that in which the two Houses shall be sitting.

Section 6 - Compensation

(The Senators and Representatives shall receive a Compensation for their Services, to be ascertained by Law, and paid out of the Treasury of the United States.) (The preceding words in parentheses were modified by the 27th Amendment.) They shall in all Cases, except Treason, Felony and Breach of the Peace, be privileged from Arrest during their Attendance at the Session of their respective Houses, and in going to and returning from the same; and for any Speech or Debate in either House, they shall not be questioned in any other Place.

No Senator or Representative shall, during the Time for which he was elected, be appointed to any civil Office under the Authority of the United States which shall have been created, or the Emoluments whereof shall have been increased during such time; and no Person holding any Office under the United States, shall be a Member of either House during his Continuance in Office.

Section 7 - Revenue Bills, Legislative Process, Presidential Veto

All bills for raising Revenue shall originate in the House of Representatives; but the Senate may propose or concur with Amendments as on other Bills.

Every Bill which shall have passed the House of Representatives and the Senate, shall, before it become a Law, be presented to the President of the United States; If he approve he shall sign it, but if not he shall return it, with his Objections to that House in which it shall have originated, who shall enter the Objections at large on their Journal, and proceed to reconsider it. If after such Reconsideration two thirds of that House shall agree to pass the Bill, it shall be sent, together with the Objections, to the other House, by which it shall likewise be reconsidered, and if approved by two thirds of that House, it shall become a Law. But in all such Cases the Votes of both Houses shall be determined by Yeas and Nays, and the Names of the Persons voting for and against the Bill shall be entered on the Journal of each House respectively. If any Bill shall not be returned by the President within ten Days (Sundays excepted) after it shall have been presented to him, the Same shall be a Law, in like Manner as if he had signed it, unless the Congress by their Adjournment prevent its Return, in which Case it shall not be a Law.

Every Order, Resolution, or Vote to which the Concurrence of the Senate and House of Representatives may be necessary (except on a question of Adjournment) shall be presented to the President of the United States; and before the Same shall take Effect, shall be approved by him, or being disapproved by him, shall be repassed by two thirds of the Senate and House of Representatives, according to the Rules and Limitations prescribed in the Case of a Bill.

Section 8 - Powers of Congress

The Congress shall have Power To lay and collect Taxes, Duties, Imposts and Excises, to pay the Debts and provide for the common Defence and general Welfare of the United States; but all Duties, Imposts and Excises shall be uniform throughout the United States;

To borrow money on the credit of the United States;

To regulate Commerce with foreign Nations, and among the several States, and with the Indian Tribes;

To establish an uniform Rule of Naturalization, and uniform Laws on the subject of Bankruptcies throughout the United States;

To coin Money, regulate the Value thereof, and of foreign Coin, and fix the Standard of Weights and Measures;

To provide for the Punishment of counterfeiting the Securities and current Coin of the United States;

To establish Post Offices and Post Roads;

To promote the Progress of Science and useful Arts, by securing for limited Times to Authors and Inventors the exclusive Right to their respective Writings and Discoveries;

To constitute Tribunals inferior to the supreme Court;

To define and punish Piracies and Felonies committed on the high Seas, and Offenses against the Law of Nations;

To declare War, grant Letters of Marque and Reprisal, and make Rules concerning Captures on Land and Water;

To raise and support Armies, but no Appropriation of Money to that Use shall be for a longer Term than two Years;

To provide and maintain a Navy;

To make Rules for the Government and Regulation of the land and naval Forces;

To provide for calling forth the Militia to execute the Laws of the Union, suppress Insurrections and repel Invasions;

To provide for organizing, arming, and disciplining the Militia, and for governing such Part of them as may be employed in the Service of the United States, reserving to the States respectively, the Appointment of the Officers, and the Authority of training the Militia according to the discipline prescribed by Congress;

To exercise exclusive Legislation in all Cases whatsoever, over such District (not exceeding ten Miles square) as may, by Cession of particular States, and the acceptance of Congress, become the Seat of the Government of the United States, and to exercise like Authority over all Places purchased by the Consent of the Legislature of the State in which the Same shall be, for the Erection of Forts, Magazines, Arsenals, dock-Yards, and other needful Buildings; And

To make all Laws which shall be necessary and proper for carrying into Execution the foregoing Powers, and all other Powers vested by this Constitution in the Government of the United States, or in any Department or Officer thereof.

Section 9 - Limits on Congress

The Migration or Importation of such Persons as any of the States now existing shall think proper to admit, shall not be prohibited by the Congress prior to the Year one thousand eight hundred and eight, but a tax or duty may be imposed on such Importation, not exceeding ten dollars for each Person.

The privilege of the Writ of Habeas Corpus shall not be suspended, unless when in Cases of Rebellion or Invasion the public Safety may require it.

No Bill of Attainder or ex post facto Law shall be passed.

(No capitation, or other direct, Tax shall be laid, unless in Proportion to the Census or Enumeration herein before directed to be taken.) (Section in parentheses clarified by the 16th Amendment.)

No Tax or Duty shall be laid on Articles exported from any State.

No Preference shall be given by any Regulation of Commerce or Revenue to the Ports of one State over those of another: nor shall Vessels bound to, or from, one State, be obliged to enter, clear, or pay Duties in another.

No Money shall be drawn from the Treasury, but in Consequence of Appropriations made by Law; and a regular Statement and Account of the Receipts and Expenditures of all public Money shall be published from time to time.

No Title of Nobility shall be granted by the United States: And no Person holding any Office of Profit or Trust under them, shall, without the Consent of the Congress, accept of any present, Emolument, Office, or Title, of any kind whatever, from any King, Prince or foreign State.

Section 10 - Powers prohibited of States

No State shall enter into any Treaty, Alliance, or Confederation; grant Letters of Marque and Reprisal; coin Money; emit Bills of Credit; make any Thing but gold and silver Coin a Tender in Payment of Debts; pass any Bill of Attainder, ex post facto Law, or Law impairing the Obligation of Contracts, or grant any Title of Nobility.

No State shall, without the Consent of the Congress, lay any Imposts or Duties on Imports or Exports, except what may be absolutely necessary for executing it's inspection Laws: and the net Produce of all Duties and Imposts, laid by any State on Imports or Exports, shall be for the Use of the Treasury of the United States; and all such Laws shall be subject to the Revision and Controul of the Congress.

No State shall, without the Consent of Congress, lay

any duty of Tonnage, keep Troops, or Ships of War in time of Peace, enter into any Agreement or Compact with another State, or with a foreign Power, or engage in War, unless actually invaded, or in such imminent Danger as will not admit of delay.

ARTICLE. II. - THE EXECUTIVE BRANCH

Section 1 - The President

The executive Power shall be vested in a President of the United States of America. He shall hold his Office during the Term of four Years, and, together with the Vice-President chosen for the same Term, be elected, as follows:

Each State shall appoint, in such Manner as the Legislature thereof may direct, a Number of Electors, equal to the whole Number of Senators and Representatives to which the State may be entitled in the Congress: but no Senator or Representative, or Person holding an Office of Trust or Profit under the United States, shall be appointed an Elector.

(The Electors shall meet in their respective States, and vote by Ballot for two persons, of whom one at least shall not lie an Inhabitant of the same State with themselves. And they shall make a List of all the Persons voted for, and of the Number of Votes for each; which List they shall sign and certify, and transmit sealed to the Seat of the Government of the United States, directed to the President of the Senate. The President of the Senate shall, in the Presence of the Senate and House of Representatives, open all the Certificates, and the Votes shall then be counted. The Person having the greatest Number of Votes shall be the President, if such Number be a Majority of the whole Number of Electors appointed; and if there be more than one who have such Majority, and have an equal Number of Votes, then the House of Representatives shall immediately chuse by Ballot one of them for President; and if no Person have a Majority, then from the five highest on the List the said House shall in like Manner chuse the President. But in chusing the President, the Votes shall be taken by States, the Representation from each State having one Vote; a quorum for this Purpose shall consist of a Member or Members from two-thirds of the States, and a Majority of all the States shall be necessary to a Choice. In every Case, after the Choice of the President, the Person having the greatest Number of Votes of the Electors shall be the Vice President. But if there should remain two or more who have equal Votes, the Senate shall chuse from them by Ballot the Vice-President.) (This clause in parentheses was superseded by the 12th Amendment.)

The Congress may determine the Time of chusing the

Electors, and the Day on which they shall give their Votes; which Day shall be the same throughout the United States.

No person except a natural born Citizen, or a Citizen of the United States, at the time of the Adoption of this Constitution, shall be eligible to the Office of President; neither shall any Person be eligible to that Office who shall not have attained to the Age of thirty-five Years, and been fourteen Years a Resident within the United States.

(In Case of the Removal of the President from Office, or of his Death, Resignation, or Inability to discharge the Powers and Duties of the said Office, the same shall devolve on the Vice President, and the Congress may by Law provide for the Case of Removal, Death, Resignation or Inability, both of the President and Vice President, declaring what Officer shall then act as President, and such Officer shall act accordingly, until the Disability be removed, or a President shall be elected.) (This clause in parentheses has been modified by the 20th and 25th Amendments.)

The President shall, at stated Times, receive for his Services, a Compensation, which shall neither be increased nor diminished during the Period for which he shall have been elected, and he shall not receive within that Period any other Emolument from the United States, or any of them.

Before he enter on the Execution of his Office, he shall take the following Oath or Affirmation:

"I do solemnly swear (or affirm) that I will faithfully execute the Office of President of the United States, and will to the best of my Ability, preserve, protect and defend the Constitution of the United States."

Section 2 - Civilian Power over Military, Cabinet, Pardon Power, Appointments

The President shall be Commander in Chief of the Army and Navy of the United States, and of the Militia of the several States, when called into the actual Service of the United States; he may require the Opinion, in writing, of the principal Officer in each of the executive Departments, upon any subject relating to the Duties of their respective Offices, and he shall have Power to Grant Reprieves and Pardons for Offenses against the United States, except in Cases of Impeachment.

He shall have Power, by and with the Advice and Consent of the Senate, to make Treaties, provided two thirds of the Senators present concur; and he shall nominate, and by and with the Advice and Consent of the Senate, shall appoint Ambassadors, other public Ministers and Consuls, Judges of the supreme Court, and all other Officers of the United States, whose Appointments are not herein otherwise provided for, and which shall be established by Law: but the Congress may by Law vest the Appointment of such inferior Officers, as they think proper, in the President alone, in the Courts of Law, or in the Heads of Departments.

The President shall have Power to fill up all Vacancies that may happen during the Recess of the Senate, by granting Commissions which shall expire at the End of their next Session.

Section 3 - State of the Union, Convening Congress

He shall from time to time give to the Congress Information of the State of the Union, and recommend to their Consideration such Measures as he shall judge necessary and expedient; he may, on extraordinary Occasions, convene both Houses, or either of them, and in Case of Disagreement between them, with Respect to the Time of Adjournment, he may adjourn them to such Time as he shall think proper; he shall receive Ambassadors and other public Ministers; he shall take Care that the Laws be faithfully executed, and shall Commission all the Officers of the United States.

Section 4 - Disqualification

The President, Vice President and all civil Officers of the United States, shall be removed from Office on Impeachment for, and Conviction of, Treason, Bribery, or other high Crimes and Misdemeanors.

ARTICLE III. - THE JUDICIAL BRANCH

Section 1 - Judicial powers

The judicial Power of the United States, shall be vested in one supreme Court, and in such inferior Courts as the Congress may from time to time ordain and establish. The Judges, both of the supreme and inferior Courts, shall hold their Offices during good Behavior, and shall, at stated Times, receive for their Services a Compensation which shall not be diminished during their Continuance in Office.

Section 2 - Trial by Jury, Original Jurisdiction, Jury Trials

(The judicial Power shall extend to all Cases, in Law and Equity, arising under this Constitution, the Laws of the United States, and Treaties made, or which shall be made, under their Authority; to all Cases affecting Ambassadors, other public Ministers and Consuls; to all Cases of admiralty and maritime Jurisdiction; to Controversies to which the United States shall be a Party; to Controversies between two or more States; between a State and Citizens of another State; between Citizens of different States; between Citizens of the same State claiming Lands under Grants of different States, and between a State, or the Citizens thereof, and foreign States, Citizens or Subjects.) (This section in parentheses is modified by the 11th Amendment.)

In all Cases affecting Ambassadors, other public Ministers and Consuls, and those in which a State shall be Party, the supreme Court shall have original Jurisdiction. In all the other Cases before mentioned, the supreme Court shall have appellate Jurisdiction, both as to Law and Fact, with such Exceptions, and under such Regulations as the Congress shall make.

The Trial of all Crimes, except in Cases of Impeachment, shall be by Jury; and such Trial shall be held in the State where the said Crimes shall have been committed; but when not committed within any State, the Trial shall be at such Place or Places as the Congress may by Law have directed.

Section 3 - Treason

Treason against the United States, shall consist only in levying War against them, or in adhering to their Enemies, giving them Aid and Comfort. No Person shall be convicted of Treason unless on the Testimony of two Witnesses to the same overt Act, or on Confession in open Court.

The Congress shall have power to declare the Punishment of Treason, but no Attainder of Treason shall work Corruption of Blood, or Forfeiture except during the Life of the Person attainted.

ARTICLE. IV. - THE STATES

Section 1 - Each State to Honor all others

Full Faith and Credit shall be given in each State to the public Acts, Records, and judicial Proceedings of every other State. And the Congress may by general Laws prescribe the Manner in which such Acts, Records and Proceedings shall be proved, and the Effect thereof.

Section 2 - State citizens, Extradition

The Citizens of each State shall be entitled to all Privileges and Immunities of Citizens in the several States.

A Person charged in any State with Treason, Felony, or other Crime, who shall flee from Justice, and be found in another State, shall on demand of the executive Authority of the State from which he fled, be delivered up, to be removed to the State having Jurisdiction of the Crime.

(No Person held to Service or Labour in one State, under the Laws thereof, escaping into another, shall, in Consequence of any Law or Regulation therein, be discharged from such Service or Labour, But shall be delivered up on Claim of the Party to whom such Service or Labour may be due.) (This clause in parentheses is superseded by the 13th Amendment.)

Section 3 - New States

New States may be admitted by the Congress into this Union; but no new States shall be formed or erected within the Jurisdiction of any other State; nor any State be formed by the Junction of two or more States, or parts of States, without the Consent of the Legislatures of the States concerned as well as of the Congress.

The Congress shall have Power to dispose of and make all needful Rules and Regulations respecting the Territory or other Property belonging to the United States; and nothing in this Constitution shall be so construed as to Prejudice any Claims of the United States, or of any particular State.

Section 4 - Republican government

The United States shall guarantee to every State in this Union a Republican Form of Government, and shall protect each of them against Invasion; and on Application of the Legislature, or of the Executive (when the Legislature cannot be convened) against domestic Violence.

ARTICLE. V. - AMENDMENT

The Congress, whenever two thirds of both Houses shall deem it necessary, shall propose Amendments to this Constitution, or, on the Application of the Legislatures of two thirds of the several States, shall call a Convention for proposing Amendments, which, in either Case, shall be valid to all Intents and Purposes, as part of this Constitution, when ratified by the Legislatures of three fourths of the several States, or by Conventions in three fourths thereof, as the one or the other Mode of Ratification may be proposed by the Congress; Provided

that no Amendment which may be made prior to the
Year One thousand eight hundred and eight shall in any
Manner affect the first and fourth Clauses in the Ninth
Section of the first Article; and that no State, without its
Consent, shall be deprived of its equal Suffrage in the
Senate.

ARTICLE. VI. - DEBTS, SUPREMACY, OATHS

All Debts contracted and Engagements entered into,
before the Adoption of this Constitution, shall be as valid
against the United States under this Constitution, as under the Confederation.

This Constitution, and the Laws of the United States
which shall be made in Pursuance thereof; and all Treaties
made, or which shall be made, under the Authority of the
United States, shall be the supreme Law of the Land; and
the Judges in every State shall be bound thereby, any
Thing in the Constitution or Laws of any State to the
Contrary notwithstanding.

The Senators and Representatives before mentioned,
and the Members of the several State Legislatures, and all
executive and judicial Officers, both of the United States
and of the several States, shall be bound by Oath or Affirmation, to support this Constitution; but no religious Test
shall ever be required as a Qualification to any Office or
public Trust under the United States.

ARTICLE. VII. - RATIFICATION DOCUMENTS

The Ratification of the Conventions of nine States, shall be sufficient for the Establishment of this Constitution between the States so ratifying the Same.

Done in Convention by the Unanimous Consent of the States present the Seventeenth Day of September in the Year of our Lord one thousand seven hundred and Eighty seven and of the Independence of the United States of America the Twelfth. In Witness whereof We have hereunto subscribed our Names.

======

G.º Washington - President and deputy from Virginia

New Hampshire - John Langdon, Nicholas Gilman

Massachusetts - Nathaniel Gorham, Rufus King

Connecticut - Wm Saml Johnson, Roger Sherman

New York - Alexander Hamilton

New Jersey - Wil Livingston, David Brearley, Wm Paterson, Jona. Dayton

Pennsylvania - B Franklin, Thomas Mifflin, Robt Morris, Geo. Clymer, Thos FitzSimons, Jared Ingersoll, James Wilson, Gouv Morris

Delaware - Geo. Read, Gunning Bedford jun, John Dickinson,

Richard Bassett, Jaco. Broom

Maryland - James McHenry, Dan of St Tho Jenifer, Danl Carroll

Virginia - John Blair, James Madison Jr.

North Carolina - Wm Blount, Richd Dobbs Spaight, Hu Williamson

South Carolina - J. Rutledge, Charles Cotesworth Pinckney, Charles Pinckney, Pierce Butler

Georgia - William Few, Abr Baldwin

Attest: William Jackson, Secretary

THE AMENDMENTS

The following are the Amendments to the Constitution. The first ten Amendments collectively are commonly known as the Bill of Rights.

THE BILL OF RIGHTS

Congress of the United States

begun and held at the City of New-York, on

Wednesday the fourth of March, one thousand seven hundred and eighty nine.

Preamble: THE Conventions of a number of the States, having at the time of their adopting the Constitution, expressed a desire, in order to prevent misconstruction or abuse of its powers, that further declaratory and restrictive clauses should be added: And as extending the ground of public confidence in the Government, will best ensure the beneficent ends of its institution.

RESOLVED by the Senate and House of Representatives of the United States of America, in Congress assembled, two thirds of both Houses concurring, that the following Articles be proposed to the Legislatures of the several States, as amendments to the Constitution of the United States, all, or any of which Articles, when ratified by three fourths of the said Legislatures, to be valid to all intents and purposes, as part of the said Constitution; viz.

ARTICLES in addition to, and Amendment of the Constitution of the United States of America, proposed by Congress, and ratified by the Legislatures of the several States, pursuant to the fifth Article of the original Constitution.

Amendment 1 - Freedom of Religion, Press, Expression. Ratified 12/15/1791.

Congress shall make no law respecting an establishment of religion, or prohibiting the free exercise thereof; or abridging the freedom of speech, or of the press; or the right of the people peaceably to assemble, and to petition the Government for a redress of grievances.

Amendment 2 - Right to Bear Arms. Ratified 12/15/1791.

A well regulated Militia, being necessary to the security of a free State, the right of the people to keep and bear Arms, shall not be infringed.

Amendment 3 - Quartering of Soldiers. Ratified 12/15/1791.

No Soldier shall, in time of peace be quartered in any house, without the consent of the Owner, nor in time of war, but in a manner to be prescribed by law.

Amendment 4 - Search and Seizure. Ratified 12/15/1791.

The right of the people to be secure in their persons, houses, papers, and effects, against unreasonable searches and seizures, shall not be violated, and no Warrants shall issue, but upon probable cause, supported by Oath or affirmation, and particularly describing the place to be searched, and the persons or things to be seized.

Amendment 5 - Trial and Punishment, Compensation for Takings. Ratified 12/15/1791.

No person shall be held to answer for a capital, or otherwise infamous crime, unless on a presentment or indictment of a Grand Jury, except in cases arising in the land or naval forces, or in the Militia, when in actual service in time of War or public danger; nor shall any person be subject for the same offense to be twice put in jeopardy of life or limb; nor shall be compelled in any criminal case to be a witness against himself, nor be deprived of life, liberty, or property, without due process of law; nor shall private property be taken for public use, without just compensation.

Amendment 6 - Right to Speedy Trial, Confrontation of Witnesses. Ratified 12/15/1791.

In all criminal prosecutions, the accused shall enjoy the right to a speedy and public trial, by an impartial jury of the State and district wherein the crime shall have been committed, which district shall have been previously ascertained by law, and to be informed of the nature and cause of the accusation; to be confronted with the witnesses against him; to have compulsory process for obtaining witnesses in his favor, and to have the Assistance of Counsel for his defence.

Amendment 7 - Trial by Jury in Civil Cases. Ratified 12/15/1791.

In Suits at common law, where the value in controversy shall exceed twenty dollars, the right of trial by jury shall be preserved, and no fact tried by a jury, shall be otherwise re-examined in any Court of the United States, than according to the rules of the common law.

Amendment 8 - Cruel and Unusual Punishment. Ratified 12/15/1791.

Excessive bail shall not be required, nor excessive fines imposed, nor cruel and unusual punishments inflicted.

Amendment 9 - Construction of Constitution. Ratified 12/15/1791.

The enumeration in the Constitution, of certain rights, shall not be construed to deny or disparage others retained by the people.

Amendment 10 - Powers of the States and People. Ratified 12/15/1791.

The powers not delegated to the United States by the Constitution, nor prohibited by it to the States, are reserved to the States respectively, or to the people.

ADDITIONAL AMENDMENTS

Amendment 11 - Judicial Limits. Ratified 2/7/1795.

The Judicial power of the United States shall not be construed to extend to any suit in law or equity, commenced or prosecuted against one of the United States by Citizens of another State, or by Citizens or Subjects of any Foreign State.

Amendment 12 - Choosing the President, Vice-President. Ratified 6/15/1804.

The Electors shall meet in their respective states, and vote by ballot for President and Vice-President, one of whom, at least, shall not be an inhabitant of the same state with themselves; they shall name in their ballots the person voted for as President, and in distinct ballots the person voted for as Vice-President, and they shall make distinct lists of all persons voted for as President, and of all persons voted for as Vice-President and of the number of votes for each, which lists they shall sign and certify, and transmit sealed to the seat of the government of the United States, directed to the President of the Senate;

The President of the Senate shall, in the presence of the Senate and House of Representatives, open all the certificates and the votes shall then be counted;

The person having the greatest Number of votes for President, shall be the President, if such number be a majority of the whole number of Electors appointed; and if no person have such majority, then from the persons having the highest numbers not exceeding three on the list of those voted for as President, the House of Representatives shall choose immediately, by ballot, the President. But in choosing the President, the votes shall be taken by states, the representation from each state having one vote; a quorum for this purpose shall consist of a member or members from two-thirds of the states, and a majority of all the states shall be necessary to a choice. And if the House of Representatives shall not choose a President whenever the right of choice shall devolve upon them, before the fourth day of March next following, then the Vice-President shall act as President, as in the case of the death or other constitutional disability of the President.

The person having the greatest number of votes as Vice-President, shall be the Vice-President, if such number be a majority of the whole number of Electors appointed, and if no person have a majority, then from the two highest numbers on the list, the Senate shall choose the Vice-President; a quorum for the purpose shall consist of two-thirds of the whole number of Senators, and a majority of the whole number shall be necessary to a choice. But no person constitutionally ineligible to the office of President shall be eligible to that of Vice-President of the United States.

Amendment 13 - Slavery Abolished. Ratified 12/6/1865.

1. Neither slavery nor involuntary servitude, except as a punishment for crime whereof the party shall have been duly convicted, shall exist within the United States, or any place subject to their jurisdiction.

2. Congress shall have power to enforce this article by appropriate legislation.

Amendment 14 - Citizenship Rights. Ratified 7/9/1868.

1. All persons born or naturalized in the United States, and subject to the jurisdiction thereof, are citizens of the United States and of the State wherein they reside. No State shall make or enforce any law which shall abridge the privileges or immunities of citizens of the United States; nor shall any State deprive any person of life, liberty, or property, without due process of law; nor deny to any person within its jurisdiction the equal protection of the laws.

2. Representatives shall be apportioned among the several States according to their respective numbers, counting the whole number of persons in each State, excluding Indians not taxed. But when the right to vote at any election for the choice of electors for President and Vice-President of the United States, Representatives in Congress, the Executive and Judicial officers of a State, or the members of the Legislature thereof, is denied to any of the male inhabitants of such State, being twenty-one years of age, and citizens of the United States, or in any way abridged, except for participation in rebellion, or other crime, the basis of representation therein shall be reduced in the proportion which the number of such male citizens shall bear to the whole number of male citizens twenty-one years of age in such State.

3. No person shall be a Senator or Representative in Congress, or elector of President and Vice-President, or hold any office, civil or military, under the United States, or under any State, who, having previously taken an oath, as a member of Congress, or as an officer of the United States, or as a member of any State legislature, or as an executive or judicial officer of any State, to support the Constitution of the United States, shall have engaged in insurrection or rebellion against the same, or given aid or comfort to the enemies thereof. But Congress may by a vote of two-thirds of each House, remove such disability.

4. The validity of the public debt of the United States, authorized by law, including debts incurred for payment of pensions and bounties for services in suppressing insurrection or rebellion, shall not be questioned. But neither the United States nor any State shall assume or pay any debt or obligation incurred in aid of insurrection or rebellion against the United States, or any claim for the loss or emancipation of any slave; but all such debts, obligations and claims shall be held illegal and void.

5. The Congress shall have power to enforce, by appropriate legislation, the provisions of this article.

Amendment 15 - Race No Bar to Vote. Ratified 2/3/1870.

1. The right of citizens of the United States to vote shall not be denied or abridged by the United States or by any

State on account of race, color, or previous condition of servitude.

2. The Congress shall have power to enforce this article by appropriate legislation.

Amendment 16 - Status of Income Tax Clarified. Ratified 2/3/1913.

The Congress shall have power to lay and collect taxes on incomes, from whatever source derived, without apportionment among the several States, and without regard to any census or enumeration.

Amendment 17 - Senators Elected by Popular Vote. Ratified 4/8/1913.

The Senate of the United States shall be composed of two Senators from each State, elected by the people thereof, for six years; and each Senator shall have one vote. The electors in each State shall have the qualifications requisite for electors of the most numerous branch of the State legislatures.

When vacancies happen in the representation of any State in the Senate, the executive authority of such State shall issue writs of election to fill such vacancies: Provided, That the legislature of any State may empower the executive thereof to make temporary appointments until the people fill the vacancies by election as the legislature may direct.

This amendment shall not be so construed as to affect the election or term of any Senator chosen before it becomes valid as part of the Constitution.

Amendment 18 - Liquor Abolished. Ratified 1/16/1919. Repealed by Amendment 21, 12/5/1933.

1. After one year from the ratification of this article the manufacture, sale, or transportation of intoxicating liquors within, the importation thereof into, or the exportation thereof from the United States and all territory subject to the jurisdiction thereof for beverage purposes is hereby prohibited.

2. The Congress and the several States shall have concurrent power to enforce this article by appropriate legislation.

3. This article shall be inoperative unless it shall have been ratified as an amendment to the Constitution by the legislatures of the several States, as provided in the Constitution, within seven years from the date of the submission hereof to the States by the Congress.

Amendment 19 - Women's Suffrage. Ratified 8/18/1920.

The right of citizens of the United States to vote shall not be denied or abridged by the United States or by any State on account of sex.

Congress shall have power to enforce this article by appropriate legislation.

Amendment 20 - Presidential, Congressional Terms. Ratified 1/23/1933.

1. The terms of the President and Vice President shall end at noon on the 20th day of January, and the terms of Senators and Representatives at noon on the 3d day of January, of the years in which such terms would have ended if this article had not been ratified; and the terms of their successors shall then begin.

2. The Congress shall assemble at least once in every year, and such meeting shall begin at noon on the 3d day of January, unless they shall by law appoint a different day.

3. If, at the time fixed for the beginning of the term of the President, the President elect shall have died, the Vice President elect shall become President. If a President shall not have been chosen before the time fixed for the beginning of his term, or if the President elect shall have failed to qualify, then the Vice President elect shall act as President until a President shall have qualified; and the Congress may by law provide for the case wherein neither a President elect nor a Vice President elect shall have qualified, declaring who shall then act as President, or the manner in which one who is to act shall be selected, and such person shall act accordingly until a President or Vice President shall have qualified.

4. The Congress may by law provide for the case of the death of any of the persons from whom the House of Representatives may choose a President whenever the right of choice shall have devolved upon them, and for the case of the death of any of the persons from whom the Senate may choose a Vice President whenever the right of choice shall have devolved upon them.

5. Sections 1 and 2 shall take effect on the 15th day of October following the ratification of this article.

6. This article shall be inoperative unless it shall have been ratified as an amendment to the Constitution by the legislatures of three-fourths of the several States within seven years from the date of its submission.

Amendment 21 - Amendment 18 Repealed. Ratified 12/5/1933.

1. The eighteenth article of amendment to the Constitution of the United States is hereby repealed.

2. The transportation or importation into any State, Territory, or possession of the United States for delivery or use therein of intoxicating liquors, in violation of the laws thereof, is hereby prohibited.

3. The article shall be inoperative unless it shall have been ratified as an amendment to the Constitution by conventions in the several States, as provided in the Constitution, within seven years from the date of the submission hereof to the States by the Congress.

Amendment 22 - Presidential Term Limits. Ratified 2/27/1951.

1. No person shall be elected to the office of the President more than twice, and no person who has held the office of President, or acted as President, for more than two years of a term to which some other person was elected President shall be elected to the office of the President more than once. But this Article shall not apply to any person holding the office of President, when this Article was proposed by the Congress, and shall not prevent any person who may be holding the office of President, or acting as President, during the term within which this Article becomes operative from holding the office of President or acting as President during the remainder of such term.

2. This article shall be inoperative unless it shall have been ratified as an amendment to the Constitution by the legislatures of three-fourths of the several States within seven years from the date of its submission to the States by the Congress.

Amendment 23 - Presidential Vote for District of Columbia. Ratified 3/29/1961.

1. The District constituting the seat of Government of the United States shall appoint in such manner as the Congress may direct: A number of electors of President and Vice President equal to the whole number of Senators and Representatives in Congress to which the Dis-

trict would be entitled if it were a State, but in no event more than the least populous State; they shall be in addition to those appointed by the States, but they shall be considered, for the purposes of the election of President and Vice President, to be electors appointed by a State; and they shall meet in the District and perform such duties as provided by the twelfth article of amendment.

2. The Congress shall have power to enforce this article by appropriate legislation.

Amendment 24 - Poll Tax Barred. Ratified 1/23/1964.

1. The right of citizens of the United States to vote in any primary or other election for President or Vice President, for electors for President or Vice President, or for Senator or Representative in Congress, shall not be denied or abridged by the United States or any State by reason of failure to pay any poll tax or other tax.

2. The Congress shall have power to enforce this article by appropriate legislation.

Amendment 25 - Presidential Disability and Succession. Ratified 2/10/1967.

1. In case of the removal of the President from office or of his death or resignation, the Vice President shall become President.

2. Whenever there is a vacancy in the office of the Vice President, the President shall nominate a Vice President

who shall take office upon confirmation by a majority vote of both Houses of Congress.

3. Whenever the President transmits to the President pro tempore of the Senate and the Speaker of the House of Representatives his written declaration that he is unable to discharge the powers and duties of his office, and until he transmits to them a written declaration to the contrary, such powers and duties shall be discharged by the Vice President as Acting President.

4. Whenever the Vice President and a majority of either the principal officers of the executive departments or of such other body as Congress may by law provide, transmit to the President pro tempore of the Senate and the Speaker of the House of Representatives their written declaration that the President is unable to discharge the powers and duties of his office, the Vice President shall immediately assume the powers and duties of the office as Acting President.

Thereafter, when the President transmits to the President pro tempore of the Senate and the Speaker of the House of Representatives his written declaration that no inability exists, he shall resume the powers and duties of his office unless the Vice President and a majority of either the principal officers of the executive department or of such other body as Congress may by law provide, transmit within four days to the President pro tempore of the Senate and the Speaker of the House of Representatives their written declaration that the President is unable to discharge the powers and duties of his office. Thereupon Congress shall decide the issue, assembling within forty eight hours for that purpose if not in session. If the Congress, within twenty one days after receipt of the latter written declaration, or, if Congress is not in session, within twenty one days after Congress is required to assemble, determines by two thirds vote of both Houses that the President is unable to discharge the powers and duties of his office, the Vice President shall continue to discharge the same as Acting President; otherwise, the President shall resume the powers and duties of his office.

Amendment 26 - Voting Age Set to 18 Years. Ratified 7/1/1971.

1. The right of citizens of the United States, who are eighteen years of age or older, to vote shall not be denied or abridged by the United States or by any State on account of age.

2. The Congress shall have power to enforce this article by appropriate legislation.

Amendment 27 - Limiting Congressional Pay Increases. Ratified 5/7/1992.

No law, varying the compensation for the services of the Senators and Representatives, shall take effect, until an election of Representatives shall have intervened.

GEORGE WASHINGTON: FIRST INAUGU-RAL ADDRESS

In the City of New York

Thursday, April 30, 1789

The Nation's first chief executive took his oath of office in April in New York City on the balcony of the Senate Chamber at Federal Hall on Wall Street. General Washington had been unanimously elected President by the first electoral college, and John Adams was elected Vice President because he received the second greatest number of votes. Under the rules, each elector cast two votes. The Chancellor of New York and fellow Freemason, Robert R. Livingston administered the oath of office. The Bible on which the oath was sworn belonged to New York's St. John's Masonic Lodge. The new President gave his inaugural address before a joint session of the two Houses of Congress assembled inside the Senate Chamber.

Fellow-Citizens of the Senate and of the House of Representatives:

AMONG the vicissitudes incident to life no event could have filled me with greater anxieties than that of which the notification was transmitted by your order, and received on the 14th day of the present month. On the one hand, I was summoned by my country, whose voice I can never hear but with veneration and love, from a retreat which I had chosen with the fondest predilection, and, in my flattering hopes, with an immutable decision, as the asylum of my declining years—a retreat which was rendered every day more necessary as well as more dear to me by the addition of habit to inclination, and of frequent interruptions in my health to the gradual waste committed on it by time. On the other hand, the magnitude and difficulty of the trust to which the voice of my country called me, being sufficient to awaken in the wisest and most experienced of her citizens a distrustful scrutiny into his qualifications, could not but overwhelm with despondence one who (inheriting inferior endowments from nature and unpracticed in the duties of civil administration) ought to be peculiarly conscious of his own deficiencies. In this conflict of emotions all I dare aver is that it has been my faithful study to collect my duty from a just appreciation of every circumstance by which it might be affected. All I dare hope is that if, in executing this task, I have been too much swayed by a grateful remembrance of former instances, or by an affectionate sensibility to this transcendent proof of the confidence of my fellow-citizens, and have thence too little consulted my incapacity as well as disinclination for the weighty and untried cares before me, my error will be palliated by the motives which mislead me, and its consequences be judged by my country with some share of the partiality in which they originated.

1. Such being the impressions under which I have, in obedience to the public summons, repaired to the present station, it would be peculiarly improper to omit in this first official act my fervent supplications to that Almighty Being who rules over the universe, who presides in the councils of nations, and whose providential aids can supply every human defect, that His benediction may consecrate to the liberties and happiness of the people of the United States a Government instituted by themselves for these essential purposes, and may enable every instrument employed in its administration to execute with success the functions allotted to his charge. In tendering this homage to the Great Author of every public and private good, I assure myself that it expresses your sentiments not less than my own, nor those of my fellow-citizens at large less than either. No people can be bound to acknowledge and adore the Invisible Hand which conducts the affairs of men more than those of the United States. Every step by which they have advanced to the character of an independent nation seems to have been distinguished by some token of providential agency; and in the important revolution just accomplished in the system of their united government the tranquil deliberations and voluntary consent of so many distinct communities from which the event has resulted can not be compared with the means by which most governments have been established without some return of pious gratitude, along with an humble anticipation of the future blessings which the past seem to

presage. These reflections, arising out of the present crisis, have forced themselves too strongly on my mind to be suppressed. You will join with me, I trust, in thinking that there are none under the influence of which the proceedings of a new and free government can more auspiciously commence.

2. By the article establishing the executive department it is made the duty of the President "to recommend to your consideration such measures as he shall judge necessary and expedient." The circumstances under which I now meet you will acquit me from entering into that subject further than to refer to the great constitutional charter under which you are assembled, and which, in defining your powers, designates the objects to which your attention is to be given. It will be more consistent with those circumstances, and far more congenial with the feelings which actuate me, to substitute, in place of a recommendation of particular measures, the tribute that is due to the talents, the rectitude, and the patriotism which adorn the characters selected to devise and adopt them. In these honorable qualifications I behold the surest pledges that as on one side no local prejudices or attachments, no separate views nor party animosities, will misdirect the comprehensive and equal eye which ought to watch over this great assemblage of communities and interests, so, on another, that the foundation of our national policy will be laid in the pure and immutable principles of private mo-

rality, and the preeminence of free government be exemplified by all the attributes which can win the affections of its citizens and command the respect of the world. I dwell on this prospect with every satisfaction which an ardent love for my country can inspire, since there is no truth more thoroughly established than that there exists in the economy and course of nature an indissoluble union between virtue and happiness; between duty and advantage; between the genuine maxims of an honest and magnanimous policy and the solid rewards of public prosperity and felicity; since we ought to be no less persuaded that the propitious smiles of Heaven can never be expected on a nation that disregards the eternal rules of order and right which Heaven itself has ordained; and since the preservation of the sacred fire of liberty and the destiny of the republican model of government are justly considered, perhaps, as deeply, as finally, staked on the experiment entrusted to the hands of the American people.

3. Besides the ordinary objects submitted to your care, it will remain with your judgment to decide how far an exercise of the occasional power delegated by the fifth article of the Constitution is rendered expedient at the present juncture by the nature of objections which have been urged against the system, or by the degree of inquietude which has given birth to them. Instead of undertaking particular recommendations on this subject, in which I could be guided by no lights derived from official opportunities, I shall again give way to my entire confidence in

your discernment and pursuit of the public good; for I assure myself that whilst you carefully avoid every alteration which might endanger the benefits of an united and effective government, or which ought to await the future lessons of experience, a reverence for the characteristic rights of freemen and a regard for the public harmony will sufficiently influence your deliberations on the question how far the former can be impregnably fortified or the latter be safely and advantageously promoted.

4. To the foregoing observations I have one to add, which will be most properly addressed to the House of Representatives. It concerns myself, and will therefore be as brief as possible. When I was first honored with a call into the service of my country, then on the eve of an arduous struggle for its liberties, the light in which I contemplated my duty required that I should renounce every pecuniary compensation. From this resolution I have in no instance departed; and being still under the impressions which produced it, I must decline as inapplicable to myself any share in the personal emoluments which may be indispensably included in a permanent provision for the executive department, and must accordingly pray that the pecuniary estimates for the station in which I am placed may during my continuance in it be limited to such actual expenditures as the public good may be thought to require.

5. Having thus imparted to you my sentiments as they have been awakened by the occasion which brings us

together, I shall take my present leave; but not without resorting once more to the benign Parent of the Human Race in humble supplication that, since He has been pleased to favor the American people with opportunities for deliberating in perfect tranquillity, and dispositions for deciding with unparalleled unanimity on a form of government for the security of their union and the advancement of their happiness, so His divine blessing may be equally conspicuous in the enlarged views, the temperate consultations, and the wise measures on which the success of this Government must depend.

WASHINGTON'S FAREWELL ADDRESS, 1796

Friends and Citizens:

The period for a new election of a citizen to administer the executive government of the United States being not far distant, and the time actually arrived when your thoughts must be employed in designating the person who is to be clothed with that important trust, it appears to me proper, especially as it may conduce to a more distinct expression of the public voice, that I should now apprise you of the resolution I have formed, to decline being considered among the number of those out of whom a choice is to be made.

I beg you, at the same time, to do me the justice to be assured that this resolution has not been taken without a strict regard to all the considerations appertaining to the relation which binds a dutiful citizen to his country; and that in withdrawing the tender of service, which silence in my situation might imply, I am influenced by no diminution of zeal for your future interest, no deficiency of grateful respect for your past kindness, but am supported by a full conviction that the step is compatible with both.

The acceptance of, and continuance hitherto in, the office to which your suffrages have twice called me have been a uniform sacrifice of inclination to the opinion of duty and to a deference for what appeared to be your desire. I constantly hoped that it would have been much earlier in my power, consistently with motives which I was not at liberty to disregard, to return to that retirement from which I had been reluctantly drawn. The strength of my inclination to do this, previous to the last election, had even led to the preparation of an address to declare it to you; but mature reflection on the then perplexed and critical posture of our affairs with foreign nations, and the unanimous advice of persons entitled to my confidence, impelled me to abandon the idea.

I rejoice that the state of your concerns, external as well as internal, no longer renders the pursuit of inclination incompatible with the sentiment of duty or propriety, and am persuaded, whatever partiality may be retained for my services, that, in the present circumstances of our country, you will not disapprove my determination to retire.

The impressions with which I first undertook the arduous trust were explained on the proper occasion. In the discharge of this trust, I will only say that I have, with good intentions, contributed towards the organization and administration of the government the best exertions of which a very fallible judgment was capable. Not unconscious in the outset of the inferiority of my qualifications, experience in my own eyes, perhaps still more in the eyes of others, has strengthened the motives to diffidence of myself; and every day the increasing weight of years admonishes me more and more that the shade of retirement is as necessary to me as it will be welcome. Satisfied that if any circumstances have given peculiar value to my services, they were temporary, I have the consolation to believe that, while choice and prudence invite me to quit the political scene, patriotism does not forbid it.

In looking forward to the moment which is intended to terminate the career of my public life, my feelings do not permit me to suspend the deep acknowledgment of that debt of gratitude which I owe to my beloved country for the many honors it has conferred upon me; still more for the steadfast confidence with which it has supported me; and for the opportunities I have thence enjoyed of manifesting my inviolable attachment, by services faithful and persevering, though in usefulness unequal to my zeal. If benefits have resulted to our country from these services, let it always be remembered to your praise, and as

an instructive example in our annals, that under circumstances in which the passions, agitated in every direction,
were liable to mislead, amidst appearances sometimes
dubious, vicissitudes of fortune often discouraging, in
situations in which not unfrequently want of success has
countenanced the spirit of criticism, the constancy of
your support was the essential prop of the efforts, and a
guarantee of the plans by which they were effected. Pro-
foundly penetrated with this idea, I shall carry it with me
to my grave, as a strong incitement to unceasing vows
that heaven may continue to you the choicest tokens of
its beneficence; that your union and brotherly affection
may be perpetual; that the free Constitution, which is the
work of your hands, may be sacredly maintained; that its
administration in every department may be stamped with
wisdom and virtue; that, in fine, the happiness of the people of these States, under the auspices of liberty, may be
made complete by so careful a preservation and so pru-
dent a use of this blessing as will acquire to them the
glory of recommending it to the applause, the affection,
and adoption of every nation which is yet a stranger to it.

Here, perhaps, I ought to stop. But a solicitude for
your welfare, which cannot end but with my life, and the
apprehension of danger, natural to that solicitude, urge
me, on an occasion like the present, to offer to your solemn contemplation, and to recommend to your frequent
review, some sentiments which are the result of much
reflection, of no inconsiderable observation, and which

appear to me all-important to the permanency of your felicity as a people. These will be offered to you with the more freedom, as you can only see in them the disinterested warnings of a parting friend, who can possibly have no personal motive to bias his counsel. Nor can I forget, as an encouragement to it, your indulgent reception of my sentiments on a former and not dissimilar occasion.

Interwoven as is the love of liberty with every ligament of your hearts, no recommendation of mine is necessary to fortify or confirm the attachment.

The unity of government which constitutes you one people is also now dear to you. It is justly so, for it is a main pillar in the edifice of your real independence, the support of your tranquility at home, your peace abroad; of your safety; of your prosperity; of that very liberty which you so highly prize. But as it is easy to foresee that, from different causes and from different quarters, much pains will be taken, many artifices employed to weaken in your minds the conviction of this truth; as this is the point in your political fortress against which the batteries of internal and external enemies will be most constantly and actively (though often covertly and insidiously) directed, it is of infinite moment that you should properly estimate the immense value of your national union to your collective and individual happiness; that you should cherish a cordial, habitual, and immovable attachment to it; accustoming yourselves to think and speak of it as of the palladium of your political safety and prosperity; watching for its

preservation with jealous anxiety; discountenancing whatever may suggest even a suspicion that it can in any event
be abandoned; and indignantly frowning upon the first
dawning of every attempt to alienate any portion of our
country from the rest, or to enfeeble the sacred ties which
now link together the various parts.

For this you have every inducement of sympathy and
interest. Citizens, by birth or choice, of a common country, that country has a right to concentrate your affections. The name of American, which belongs to you in
your national capacity, must always exalt the just pride of
patriotism more than any appellation derived from local
discriminations. With slight shades of difference, you
have the same religion, manners, habits, and political
principles. You have in a common cause fought and tri-
umphed together; the independence and liberty you possess are the work of joint counsels, and joint efforts of
common dangers, sufferings, and successes.

But these considerations, however powerfully they
address themselves to your sensibility, are greatly out-
weighed by those which apply more immediately to your
interest. Here every portion of our country finds the most
commanding motives for carefully guarding and preserving the union of the whole.

The North, in an unrestrained intercourse with the
South, protected by the equal laws of a common government, finds in the productions of the latter great addi-

tional resources of maritime and commercial enterprise and precious materials of manufacturing industry. The South, in the same intercourse, benefiting by the agency of the North, sees its agriculture grow and its commerce expand. Turning partly into its own channels the seamen of the North, it finds its particular navigation invigorated; and, while it contributes, in different ways, to nourish and increase the general mass of the national navigation, it looks forward to the protection of a maritime strength, to which itself is unequally adapted. The East, in a like intercourse with the West, already finds, and in the progressive improvement of interior communications by land and water, will more and more find a valuable vent for the commodities which it brings from abroad, or manufactures at home. The West derives from the East supplies requisite to its growth and comfort, and, what is perhaps of still greater consequence, it must of necessity owe the secure enjoyment of indispensable outlets for its own productions to the weight, influence, and the future maritime strength of the Atlantic side of the Union, directed by an indissoluble community of interest as one nation. Any other tenure by which the West can hold this essential advantage, whether derived from its own separate strength, or from an apostate and unnatural connection with any foreign power, must be intrinsically precarious.

While, then, every part of our country thus feels an immediate and particular interest in union, all the parts combined cannot fail to find in the united mass of means and efforts greater strength, greater resource, proportionally greater security from external danger, a less frequent interruption of their peace by foreign nations; and, what is of inestimable value, they must derive from union an exemption from those broils and wars between themselves, which so frequently afflict neighboring countries not tied together by the same governments, which their own rival ships alone would be sufficient to produce, but which opposite foreign alliances, attachments, and intrigues would stimulate and embitter. Hence, likewise, they will avoid the necessity of those overgrown military establishments which, under any form of government, are inauspicious to liberty, and which are to be regarded as particularly hostile to republican liberty. In this sense it is that your union ought to be considered as a main prop of your liberty, and that the love of the one ought to endear to you the preservation of the other.

These considerations speak a persuasive language to every reflecting and virtuous mind, and exhibit the continuance of the Union as a primary object of patriotic desire. Is there a doubt whether a common government can embrace so large a sphere? Let experience solve it. To listen to mere speculation in such a case were criminal. We are authorized to hope that a proper organization of the whole with the auxiliary agency of governments for the respective subdivisions, will afford a happy issue to the experiment. It is well worth a fair and full experiment. With such powerful and obvious motives to union, affecting all parts of our country, while experience shall not have demonstrated its impracticability, there will always be reason to distrust the patriotism of those who in any quarter may endeavor to weaken its bands.

In contemplating the causes which may disturb our Union, it occurs as matter of serious concern that any ground should have been furnished for characterizing parties by geographical discriminations, Northern and Southern, Atlantic and Western; whence designing men may endeavor to excite a belief that there is a real difference of local interests and views. One of the expedients of party to acquire influence within particular districts is to misrepresent the opinions and aims of other districts. You cannot shield yourselves too much against the jealousies and heartburnings which spring from these misrepresentations; they tend to render alien to each other those who ought to be bound together by fraternal affection. The inhabitants of our Western country have lately had a useful lesson on this head; they have seen, in the negotiation by the Executive, and in the unanimous ratification by the Senate, of the treaty with Spain, and in the universal satisfaction at that event, throughout the United States, a decisive proof how unfounded were the suspicions propagated among them of a policy in the General Government and in the Atlantic States unfriendly to their interests in regard to the Mississippi; they have been witnesses to the formation of two treaties, that with Great Britain, and that with Spain, which secure to them everything they could desire, in respect to our foreign relations, towards confirming their prosperity. Will it not be their wisdom to rely for the preservation of these advantages on the Union by which they were procured ? Will they not henceforth be deaf to those advisers, if such there are, who would sever them from their brethren and connect them with aliens?

To the efficacy and permanency of your Union, a government for the whole is indispensable. No alliance, however strict, between the parts can be an adequate substitute; they must inevitably experience the infractions and interruptions which all alliances in all times have experienced. Sensible of this momentous truth, you have improved upon your first essay, by the adoption of a constitution of government better calculated than your former for an intimate union, and for the efficacious management of your common concerns. This government, the offspring of our own choice, uninfluenced and unawed, adopted upon full investigation and mature deliberation, completely free in its principles, in the distribution of its powers, uniting security with energy, and containing within itself a provision for its own amendment, has a just claim to your confidence and your support. Respect for its authority, compliance with its laws, acquiescence in its measures, are duties enjoined by the fundamental maxims of true liberty. The basis of our political systems is the right of the people to make and to alter their constitutions of government. But the Constitution which at any time exists, till changed by an explicit and authentic act of the whole people, is sacredly obligatory upon all. The very idea of the power and the right of the people to establish government presupposes the duty of every individual to obey the established government.

All obstructions to the execution of the laws, all combinations and associations, under whatever plausible character, with the real design to direct, control, counteract, or awe the regular deliberation and action of the constituted authorities, are destructive of this fundamental principle, and of fatal tendency. They serve to organize faction, to give it an artificial and extraordinary force; to put, in the place of the delegated will of the nation the will of a party, often a small but artful and enterprising minority of the community; and, according to the alternate triumphs of different parties, to make the public administration the mirror of the ill-concerted and incongruous projects of faction, rather than the organ of consistent and wholesome plans digested by common counsels and modified by mutual interests.

However combinations or associations of the above description may now and then answer popular ends, they are likely, in the course of time and things, to become potent engines, by which cunning, ambitious, and unprincipled men will be enabled to subvert the power of the people and to usurp for themselves the reins of government, destroying afterwards the very engines which have lifted them to unjust dominion.

Towards the preservation of your government, and
the permanency of your present happy state, it is requisite, not only that you steadily discountenance irregular
oppositions to its acknowledged authority, but also that
you resist with care the spirit of innovation upon its principles, however specious the pretexts. One method of
assault may be to effect, in the forms of the Constitution,
alterations which will impair the energy of the system, and
thus to undermine what cannot be directly overthrown.
In all the changes to which you may be invited, remember
that time and habit are at least as necessary to fix the true
character of governments as of other human institutions;
that experience is the surest standard by which to test the
real tendency of the existing constitution of a country;
that facility in changes, upon the credit of mere hypothesis and opinion, exposes to perpetual change, from the
endless variety of hypothesis and opinion; and remember,
especially, that for the efficient management of your common interests, in a country so extensive as ours, a government of as much vigor as is consistent with the perfect
security of liberty is indispensable. Liberty itself will find
in such a government, with powers properly distributed
and adjusted, its surest guardian. It is, indeed, little else
than a name, where the government is too feeble to with-
stand the enterprises of faction, to confine each member
of the society within the limits prescribed by the laws, and
to maintain all in the secure and tranquil enjoyment of the
rights of person and property.

I have already intimated to you the danger of parties in the State, with particular reference to the founding of them on geographical discriminations. Let me now take a more comprehensive view, and warn you in the most solemn manner against the baneful effects of the spirit of party generally.

This spirit, unfortunately, is inseparable from our nature, having its root in the strongest passions of the human mind. It exists under different shapes in all governments, more or less stifled, controlled, or repressed; but, in those of the popular form, it is seen in its greatest rankness, and is truly their worst enemy.

The alternate domination of one faction over another, sharpened by the spirit of revenge, natural to party dissension, which in different ages and countries has perpetrated the most horrid enormities, is itself a frightful despotism. But this leads at length to a more formal and permanent despotism. The disorders and miseries which result gradually incline the minds of men to seek security and repose in the absolute power of an individual; and sooner or later the chief of some prevailing faction, more able or more fortunate than his competitors, turns this disposition to the purposes of his own elevation, on the ruins of public liberty.

Without looking forward to an extremity of this kind (which nevertheless ought not to be entirely out of sight), the common and continual mischiefs of the spirit of party are sufficient to make it the interest and duty of a wise people to discourage and restrain it.

It serves always to distract the public councils and enfeeble the public administration. It agitates the community with ill-founded jealousies and false alarms, kindles the animosity of one part against another, foments occasionally riot and insurrection. It opens the door to foreign influence and corruption, which finds a facilitated access to the government itself through the channels of party passions. Thus the policy and the will of one country are subjected to the policy and will of another.

There is an opinion that parties in free countries are useful checks upon the administration of the government and serve to keep alive the spirit of liberty. This within certain limits is probably true; and in governments of a monarchical cast, patriotism may look with indulgence, if not with favor, upon the spirit of party. But in those of the popular character, in governments purely elective, it is a spirit not to be encouraged. From their natural tendency, it is certain there will always be enough of that spirit for every salutary purpose. And there being constant danger of excess, the effort ought to be by force of public opinion, to mitigate and assuage it. A fire not to be quenched, it demands a uniform vigilance to prevent its bursting into a flame, lest, instead of warming, it should consume.

It is important, likewise, that the habits of thinking in a free country should inspire caution in those entrusted with its administration, to confine themselves within their respective constitutional spheres, avoiding in the exercise of the powers of one department to encroach upon another. The spirit of encroachment tends to consolidate the powers of all the departments in one, and thus to create, whatever the form of government, a real despotism. A just estimate of that love of power, and proneness to abuse it, which predominates in the human heart, is sufficient to satisfy us of the truth of this position. The necessity of reciprocal checks in the exercise of political power, by dividing and distributing it into different depositaries, and constituting each the guardian of the public weal against invasions by the others, has been evinced by experiments ancient and modern; some of them in our country and under our own eyes. To preserve them must be as necessary as to institute them. If, in the opinion of the people, the distribution or modification of the constitutional powers be in any particular wrong, let it be corrected by an amendment in the way which the Constitution designates. But let there be no change by usurpation; for though this, in one instance, may be the instrument of good, it is the customary weapon by which free governments are destroyed. The precedent must always greatly overbalance in permanent evil any partial or transient benefit, which the use can at any time yield.

Of all the dispositions and habits which lead to political prosperity, religion and morality are indispensable supports. In vain would that man claim the tribute of patriotism, who should labor to subvert these great pillars of human happiness, these firmest props of the duties of men and citizens. The mere politician, equally with the pious man, ought to respect and to cherish them. A volume could not trace all their connections with private and public felicity. Let it simply be asked: Where is the security for property, for reputation, for life, if the sense of religious obligation desert the oaths which are the instruments of investigation in courts of justice ? And let us with caution indulge the supposition that morality can be maintained without religion. Whatever may be conceded to the influence of refined education on minds of peculiar structure, reason and experience both forbid us to expect that national morality can prevail in exclusion of religious principle.

It is substantially true that virtue or morality is a necessary spring of popular government. The rule, indeed, extends with more or less force to every species of free government. Who that is a sincere friend to it can look with indifference upon attempts to shake the foundation of the fabric?

Promote then, as an object of primary importance, institutions for the general diffusion of knowledge. In proportion as the structure of a government gives force to public opinion, it is essential that public opinion should be enlightened.

As a very important source of strength and security, cherish public credit. One method of preserving it is to use it as sparingly as possible, avoiding occasions of expense by cultivating peace, but remembering also that timely disbursements to prepare for danger frequently prevent much greater disbursements to repel it, avoiding likewise the accumulation of debt, not only by shunning occasions of expense, but by vigorous exertion in time of peace to discharge the debts which unavoidable wars may have occasioned, not ungenerously throwing upon posterity the burden which we ourselves ought to bear. The execution of these maxims belongs to your representatives, but it is necessary that public opinion should cooperate. To facilitate to them the performance of their duty, it is essential that you should practically bear in mind that towards the payment of debts there must be revenue; that to have revenue there must be taxes; that no taxes can be devised which are not more or less inconvenient and unpleasant; that the intrinsic embarrassment, inseparable from the selection of the proper objects (which is always a choice of difficulties), ought to be a decisive motive for a candid construction of the conduct of the government in making it, and for a spirit of acquiescence in the measures for obtaining revenue, which the public exigencies may at any time dictate.

Observe good faith and justice towards all nations; cultivate peace and harmony with all. Religion and morality enjoin this conduct; and can it be, that good policy does not equally enjoin it 7 It will be worthy of a free, enlightened, and at no distant period, a great nation, to give to mankind the magnanimous and too novel example of a people always guided by an exalted justice and benevolence. Who can doubt that, in the course of time and things, the fruits of such a plan would richly repay any temporary advantages which might be lost by a steady adherence to it ? Can it be that Providence has not connected the permanent felicity of a nation with its virtue ? The experiment, at least, is recommended by every sentiment which ennobles human nature. Alas! is it rendered impossible by its vices?

In the execution of such a plan, nothing is more essential than that permanent, inveterate antipathies against particular nations, and passionate attachments for others, should be excluded; and that, in place of them, just and amicable feelings towards all should be cultivated. The nation which indulges towards another a habitual hatred or a habitual fondness is in some degree a slave. It is a slave to its animosity or to its affection, either of which is sufficient to lead it astray from its duty and its interest. Antipathy in one nation against another disposes each more readily to offer insult and injury, to lay hold of slight causes of umbrage, and to be haughty and intractable, when accidental or trifling occasions of dispute occur. Hence, frequent collisions, obstinate, envenomed, and bloody contests. The nation, prompted by ill-will and resentment, sometimes impels to war the government, contrary to the best calculations of policy. The government sometimes participates in the national propensity, and adopts through passion what reason would reject; at other times it makes the animosity of the nation subservient to projects of hostility instigated by pride, ambition, and other sinister and pernicious motives. The peace often, sometimes perhaps the liberty, of nations, has been the victim.

So likewise, a passionate attachment of one nation for another produces a variety of evils. Sympathy for the favorite nation, facilitating the illusion of an imaginary common interest in cases where no real common interest exists, and infusing into one the enmities of the other, betrays the former into a participation in the quarrels and wars of the latter without adequate inducement or justification. It leads also to concessions to the favorite nation of privileges denied to others which is apt doubly to injure the nation making the concessions; by unnecessarily parting with what ought to have been retained, and by exciting jealousy, ill-will, and a disposition to retaliate, in the parties from whom equal privileges are withheld. And it gives to ambitious, corrupted, or deluded citizens (who devote themselves to the favorite nation), facility to betray or sacrifice the interests of their own country, without odium, sometimes even with popularity; gilding, with the appearances of a virtuous sense of obligation, a commendable deference for public opinion, or a laudable zeal for public good, the base or foolish compliances of ambition, corruption, or infatuation.

As avenues to foreign influence in innumerable ways, such attachments are particularly alarming to the truly enlightened and independent patriot. How many opportunities do they afford to tamper with domestic factions, to practice the arts of seduction, to mislead public opinion, to influence or awe the public councils 7 Such an attachment of a small or weak towards a great and powerful nation dooms the former to be the satellite of the latter.

Against the insidious wiles of foreign influence (I conjure you to believe me, fellow-citizens) the jealousy of a free people ought to be constantly awake, since history and experience prove that foreign influence is one of the most baneful foes of republican government. But that jealousy to be useful must be impartial; else it becomes the instrument of the very influence to be avoided, instead of a defense against it. Excessive partiality for one foreign nation and excessive dislike of another cause those whom they actuate to see danger only on one side, and serve to veil and even second the arts of influence on the other. Real patriots who may resist the intrigues of the favorite are liable to become suspected and odious, while its tools and dupes usurp the applause and confidence of the people, to surrender their interests.

The great rule of conduct for us in regard to foreign nations is in extending our commercial relations, to have with them as little political connection as possible. So far as we have already formed engagements, let them be fulfilled with perfect good faith. Here let us stop. Europe has a set of primary interests which to us have none; or a very remote relation. Hence she must be engaged in frequent controversies, the causes of which are essentially foreign to our concerns. Hence, therefore, it must be unwise in us to implicate ourselves by artificial ties in the ordinary vicissitudes of her politics, or the ordinary combinations and collisions of her friendships or enmities.

Our detached and distant situation invites and enables us to pursue a different course. If we remain one people under an efficient government. the period is not far off when we may defy material injury from external annoyance; when we may take such an attitude as will cause the neutrality we may at any time resolve upon to be scrupulously respected; when belligerent nations, under the impossibility of making acquisitions upon us, will not lightly hazard the giving us provocation; when we may choose peace or war, as our interest, guided by justice, shall counsel.

Why forego the advantages of so peculiar a situation? Why quit our own to stand upon foreign ground? Why, by interweaving our destiny with that of any part of Europe, entangle our peace and prosperity in the toils of European ambition, rivalship, interest, humor or caprice?

It is our true policy to steer clear of permanent alliances with any portion of the foreign world; so far, I mean, as we are now at liberty to do it; for let me not be understood as capable of patronizing infidelity to existing engagements. I hold the maxim no less applicable to public than to private affairs, that honesty is always the best policy. I repeat it, therefore, let those engagements be observed in their genuine sense. But, in my opinion, it is unnecessary and would be unwise to extend them.

Taking care always to keep ourselves by suitable establishments on a respectable defensive posture, we may safely trust to temporary alliances for extraordinary emergencies.

Harmony, liberal intercourse with all nations, are recommended by policy, humanity, and interest. But even our commercial policy should hold an equal and impartial hand; neither seeking nor granting exclusive favors or preferences; consulting the natural course of things; diffusing and diversifying by gentle means the streams of commerce, but forcing nothing; establishing (with powers so disposed, in order to give trade a stable course, to define the rights of our merchants, and to enable the government to support them) conventional rules of intercourse, the best that present circumstances and mutual opinion will permit, but temporary, and liable to be from time to time abandoned or varied, as experience and circumstances shall dictate; constantly keeping in view that it is folly in one nation to look for disinterested favors from another; that it must pay with a portion of its independence for whatever it may accept under that character; that, by such acceptance, it may place itself in the condition of having given equivalents for nominal favors, and yet of being reproached with ingratitude for not giving more. There can be no greater error than to expect or calculate upon real favors from nation to nation. It is an illusion, which experience must cure, which a just pride ought to discard.

In offering to you, my countrymen, these counsels of an old and affectionate friend, I dare not hope they will make the strong and lasting impression I could wish; that they will control the usual current of the passions, or prevent our nation from running the course which has hitherto marked the destiny of nations. But, if I may even flatter myself that they may be productive of some partial benefit, some occasional good; that they may now and then recur to moderate the fury of party spirit, to warn against the mischiefs of foreign intrigue, to guard against the impostures of pretended patriotism; this hope will be a full recompense for the solicitude for your welfare, by which they have been dictated.

How far in the discharge of my official duties I have been guided by the principles which have been delineated, the public records and other evidences of my conduct must witness to you and to the world. To myself, the assurance of my own conscience is, that I have at least believed myself to be guided by them.

In relation to the still subsisting war in Europe, my proclamation of the twenty-second of April, 1793, is the index of my plan. Sanctioned by your approving voice, and by that of your representatives in both houses of Congress, the spirit of that measure has continually governed me, uninfluenced by any attempts to deter or divert me from it.

After deliberate examination, with the aid of the best lights I could obtain, I was well satisfied that our country, under all the circumstances of the case, had a right to take, and was bound in duty and interest to take, a neutral position. Having taken it, I determined, as far as should depend upon me, to maintain it, with moderation, perseverance, and firmness.

The considerations which respect the right to hold this con duct, it is not necessary on this occasion to detail. I will only observe that, according to my understanding of the matter, that right, so far from being denied by any of the belligerent powers, has been virtually admitted by all.

The duty of holding a neutral conduct may be inferred, without anything more, from the obligation which justice and humanity impose on every nation, in cases in which it is free to act, to maintain inviolate the relations of peace and amity towards other nations.

The inducements of interest for observing that conduct will best be referred to your own reflections and experience. With me a predominant motive has been to endeavor to gain time to our country to settle and mature its yet recent institutions, and to progress without interruption to that degree of strength and consistency which is necessary to give it, humanly speaking, the command of its own fortunes.

Though, in reviewing the incidents of my administration, I am unconscious of intentional error, I am nevertheless too sensible of my defects not to think it probable that I may have committed many errors. Whatever they may be, I fervently beseech the Almighty to avert or mitigate the evils to which they may tend. I shall also carry with me the hope that my country will never cease to view them with indulgence; and that, after forty five years of my life dedicated to its service with an upright zeal, the faults of incompetent abilities will be consigned to oblivion, as myself must soon be to the mansions of rest.

Relying on its kindness in this as in other things, and actuated by that fervent love towards it, which is so natural to a man who views in it the native soil of himself and his progenitors for several generations, I anticipate with pleasing expectation that retreat in which I promise myself to realize, without alloy, the sweet enjoyment of partaking, in the midst of my fellow-citizens, the benign influence of good laws under a free government, the ever-favorite object of my heart, and the happy reward, as I trust, of our mutual cares, labors, and dangers.

Geo. Washington.

THOMAS JEFFERSON: FIRST INAUGURAL ADDRESS

In the Washington, D.C.

Wednesday, March 4, 1801

Chief Justice John Marshall administered the first executive oath of office ever taken in the new federal city in the new Senate Chamber (now the Old Supreme Court Chamber) of the partially built Capitol building. The outcome of the election of 1800 had been in doubt until late February because Thomas Jefferson and Aaron Burr, the two leading candidates, each had received 73 electoral votes. Consequently, the House of Representatives met in a special session to resolve the impasse, pursuant to the terms spelled out in the Constitution. After 30 hours of debate and balloting, Mr. Jefferson emerged as the President and Mr. Burr the Vice President. President John Adams, who had run unsuccessfully for a second term, left Washington on the day of the inauguration without attending the ceremony.

Friends and Fellow-Citizens:

CALLED upon to undertake the duties of the first executive office of our country, I avail myself of the presence of that portion of my fellow-citizens which is here assembled to express my grateful thanks for the favor with which they have been pleased to look toward me, to declare a sincere consciousness that the task is above my talents, and that I approach it with those anxious and awful presentiments which the greatness of the charge and the weakness of my powers so justly inspire. A rising nation, spread over a wide and fruitful land, traversing all the seas with the rich productions of their industry, engaged in commerce with nations who feel power and forget right, advancing rapidly to destinies beyond the reach of mortal eye—when I contemplate these transcendent objects, and see the honor, the happiness, and the hopes of this beloved country committed to the issue, and the auspices of this day, I shrink from the contemplation, and humble myself before the magnitude of the undertaking. Utterly, indeed, should I despair did not the presence of many whom I here see remind me that in the other high authorities provided by our Constitution I shall find resources of wisdom, of virtue, and of zeal on which to rely under all difficulties. To you, then, gentlemen, who are charged with the sovereign functions of legislation, and to those associated with you, I look with encouragement for that guidance and support which may enable us to steer with safety the vessel in which we are all embarked amidst the conflicting elements of a troubled world.

1. During the contest of opinion through which we have passed the animation of discussions and of exertions has sometimes worn an aspect which might impose on strangers unused to think freely and to speak and to write what they think; but this being now decided by the voice of the nation, announced according to the rules of the Constitution, all will, of course, arrange themselves under the will of the law, and unite in common efforts for the

common good. All, too, will bear in mind this sacred principle, that though the will of the majority is in all cases to prevail, that will to be rightful must be reasonable; that the minority possess their equal rights, which equal law must protect, and to violate would be oppression. Let us, then, fellow-citizens, unite with one heart and one mind. Let us restore to social intercourse that harmony and affection without which liberty and even life itself are but dreary things. And let us reflect that, having banished from our land that religious intolerance under which mankind so long bled and suffered, we have yet gained little if we countenance a political intolerance as despotic, as wicked, and capable of as bitter and bloody persecutions. During the throes and convulsions of the ancient world, during the agonizing spasms of infuriated man, seeking through blood and slaughter his long-lost liberty, it was not wonderful that the agitation of the billows should reach even this distant and peaceful shore; that this should be more felt and feared by some and less by others, and should divide opinions as to measures of safety. But every difference of opinion is not a difference of principle. We have called by different names brethren of the same principle. We are all Republicans, we are all Federalists. If there be any among us who would wish to dissolve this Union or to change its republican form, let them stand undisturbed as monuments of the safety with which error of opinion may be tolerated where reason is left free to combat it. I know, indeed, that some honest men fear that a republican government can not be strong, that this Government is not strong enough; but would the honest patriot, in the full tide of successful experiment, abandon a government which has so far kept us free and firm on the theoretic and visionary fear that this Government, the world's best hope, may by possibility want energy to preserve itself? I trust not. I believe this, on the contrary, the strongest Government on earth. I believe it the only one where every man, at the call of the law, would fly to the standard of the law, and would meet invasions of the public order as his own personal concern. Sometimes it is said that man can not be trusted with the government of himself. Can he, then, be trusted with the government of others? Or have we found angels in the forms of kings to govern him? Let history answer this question.

2. Let us, then, with courage and confidence pursue our own Federal and Republican principles, our attachment to union and representative government. Kindly separated by nature and a wide ocean from the exterminating havoc of one quarter of the globe; too high-minded to endure the degradations of the others; possessing a chosen country, with room enough for our descendants to the thousandth and thousandth generation; entertaining a due sense of our equal right to the use of our own faculties, to the acquisitions of our own industry, to honor and confidence from our fellow-citizens, resulting not from

birth, but from our actions and their sense of them; enlightened by a benign religion, professed, indeed, and practiced in various forms, yet all of them inculcating honesty, truth, temperance, gratitude, and the love of man; acknowledging and adoring an overruling Providence, which by all its dispensations proves that it delights in the happiness of man here and his greater happiness hereafter—with all these blessings, what more is necessary to make us a happy and a prosperous people? Still one thing more, fellow-citizens—a wise and frugal Government, which shall restrain men from injuring one another, shall leave them otherwise free to regulate their own pursuits of industry and improvement, and shall not take from the mouth of labor the bread it has earned. This is the sum of good government, and this is necessary to close the circle of our felicities.

3. About to enter, fellow-citizens, on the exercise of duties which comprehend everything dear and valuable to you, it is proper you should understand what I deem the essential principles of our Government, and consequently those which ought to shape its Administration. I will compress them within the narrowest compass they will bear, stating the general principle, but not all its limitations. Equal and exact justice to all men, of whatever state or persuasion, religious or political; peace, commerce, and honest friendship with all nations, entangling alliances with none; the support of the State governments

in all their rights, as the most competent administrations for our domestic concerns and the surest bulwarks against antirepublican tendencies; the preservation of the General Government in its whole constitutional vigor, as the sheet anchor of our peace at home and safety abroad; a jealous care of the right of election by the people—a mild and safe corrective of abuses which are lopped by the sword of revolution where peaceable remedies are unprovided; absolute acquiescence in the decisions of the majority, the vital principle of republics, from which is no appeal but to force, the vital principle and immediate parent of despotism; a well disciplined militia, our best reliance in peace and for the first moments of war, till regulars may relieve them; the supremacy of the civil over the military authority; economy in the public expense, that labor may be lightly burthened; the honest payment of our debts and sacred preservation of the public faith; encouragement of agriculture, and of commerce as its handmaid; the diffusion of information and arraignment of all abuses at the bar of the public reason; freedom of religion; freedom of the press, and freedom of person under the protection of the habeas corpus, and trial by juries impartially selected. These principles form the bright constellation which has gone before us and guided our steps through an age of revolution and reformation. The wisdom of our sages and blood of our heroes have been devoted to their attainment. They should be the creed of our political faith, the text of civic instruction, the touchstone by which to try the services of those we trust; and should we wander from them in moments of error or of alarm, let us hasten to retrace our steps and to regain the road which alone leads to peace, liberty, and safety.

4. I repair, then, fellow-citizens, to the post you have assigned me. With experience enough in subordinate offices to have seen the difficulties of this the greatest of all, I have learnt to expect that it will rarely fall to the lot of imperfect man to retire from this station with the reputation and the favor which bring him into it. Without pretensions to that high confidence you reposed in our first and greatest revolutionary character, whose preeminent services had entitled him to the first place in his country's love and destined for him the fairest page in the volume of faithful history, I ask so much confidence only as may give firmness and effect to the legal administration of your affairs. I shall often go wrong through defect of judgment. When right, I shall often be thought wrong by those whose positions will not command a view of the whole ground. I ask your indulgence for my own errors, which will never be intentional, and your support against the errors of others, who may condemn what they would not if seen in all its parts. The approbation implied by your suffrage is a great consolation to me for the past, and my future solicitude will be to retain the good opinion of those who have bestowed it in advance, to concili-

ate that of others by doing them all the good in my power, and to be instrumental to the happiness and freedom of all.

5. Relying, then, on the patronage of your good will, I advance with obedience to the work, ready to retire from it whenever you become sensible how much better choice it is in your power to make. And may that Infinite Power which rules the destinies of the universe lead our councils to what is best, and give them a favorable issue for your peace and prosperity.

SECTION II

THE EROSION OF DEMOCRACY

AND ITS RELATION TO TODAY

THE EROSION OF DEMOCRACY AND ITS RELATION TO TODAY

A: WHAT IS EROSION?

Erosion is a gradual wearing or eating away, so gradual that it is not easily detected. When something is overexposed to the elements without proper protection, it will slowly deteriorate and eventually disappear. This is also true for democracy: We are exposed to the elements of our own humanness. We need to be fully aware of this, so that we can protect and preserve what is very dear to us. The individual is the core of democracy … each and every individual equally. We must not lose sight of this.

In the older cultures around the world, the importance of their heritage was handed down from grandfather to grandson, one generation after the other. The elders keep the history and the value of their way of life alive in the hearts of the rising generation. This fire was constantly being lit and stoked.

Our country was brand new and did not have this tradition. We were the new kids on the block in the world, very busy exploring and conquering new lands. Our American culture is different, as is our family structure. We have never practiced the spirit of storytelling; the passing down of wisdom and values, of who we are, from generation to generation. Although democracy has been practiced, much time has passed, and what was sacred in the beginning has not been kept alive in the hearts of our future generations.

Most people today do not understand the consciousness, let alone the full scope of democracy, that our forefathers had intended for us to enjoy. "Of the people, for the people, and by the people" has lost a lot of its strength and meaning and is now on shaky ground. The "I" in "We" is no longer emphasized.

Today our government has become complicated, and difficult for the average citizen to understand and participate in. Democracy, for the average person, is not much more than the right to vote.

This does not have to be! However, before addressing how to fix it, some questions must be answered: What has happened to democracy? Where is it today? Where does the individual fit in? Where is our strength and passion needed, and how can we apply it?

This section covers and expands on this decline or erosion as well as the state and practice of democracy today.

* * * * *

Are we right back where we started from, a parallel to the early 1600's in England that led to the great migration filling our uncharted shores? Is it similar to the period just before our declared independence in 1776 with the great christening of the Boston Harbor? Why didn't it hold?

Let's take a look and see. We are not going to cover each and every point, but will cover enough, with enough detail to illustrate its declining path to what it is today.

We can't change yesterday, but with close inquiry into it and observing our participation or lack of participation, we can have an awakening of today. Once again we will open the doors of the "American Dream", its democracy with its freedom, liberty, happiness and safety for all.

We the people united in common cause, with this common consciousness at our core can make it happen….and quickly. Our passion is our power and can overcome any inroads of oppression and its ties to "Despotism".

Let's refresh our memory and briefly review our history. In the early 1800's, we were a now country with a new government in place. The "Bill of Rights" was now in effect. Our country was growing and our economy was beginning to prosper. We were a nation of thirteen states with territory comprising most of the land east of the Mississippi River with the exception of Florida and some of the land bordering Canada. We were a rural society very much dependent on our land for survival.

In 1803, Thomas Jefferson purchased from France land that doubled our territory extending us all the way to Oregon. We were a young country, change was happening and we were changing with it. Now there was all this land we had to settle; actually conquer. It was wild and so were we.

We still had the slavery issue to resolve. **Note**: This was discussed at the Constitutional Convention. Our forefathers recognized that slavery was contradictory to the freedom and equality of all people, but it was such a divisive issue. At that time, it would have been impossible to unite, not divide, as one nation of thirteen states. Therefore the issue of slavery was tabled, to be dealt with later.

[**Note:** They had accurately assessed the impossibility of unifying the thirteen states (twelve of them were slave-states). However, the real problem is that tabled items rarely get dealt with in a timely manner. Even though certain groups protested our hypocrisy regarding the issue of "equality," it took all the way to the Civil War to force the issue. It may not even have happened then, were it not for the possibility that the southern states might actively compete with the North for industry. (This is another book entirely.) Money, control, power and war have always been closely linked.]

Our economy was changing. We were beginning to manufacture more and more of our own goods. This was reducing our dependency on Europe for finished goods. Along with the growth of factories came the growth of our cities. With this density of people new issues would arise.

Issues were beginning to form and were in conflict with the intent of our forefathers. Were their warnings becoming prophecies? Let's see.

In the early 1800's (1803 to 1815) we were involved in the War of 1812 and the Napoleonic Wars. So much for minding our own business and not getting entangled with foreign politics. Although some of our actions were just, history shows us that this core issue is alive today; an issue that keeps raising its head and confronting us.

Well, we are moving west in a hurry to conquer our new uncharted lands that we bought from a third party (France), destroying the real owners without much consideration in the process.

Note: This driving force for more land created a strange alliance between freedom and violence with a mixture of fear and greed at its core. Repeated enough, a link-up is established. Every time freedom is mentioned, violence comes into play as part of the solution.

In freedom; to be free there is no conflict, therefore no violence exists. We are at peace; otherwise, we would not be free. To preserve this freedom we tend to choose violence. This becoming violent destroys the very freedom we were trying to protect. This is not just our history, but, the history of the world proves this time and time again. Our forefathers warned us about our humanness and there is violence in our humanness. If we are aware of this; call it what it is, we can, through our choices, better balance this, creating a new consciousness where we begin to employ non-violent or peaceful solutions. This does not work 100% of the time, but, is a major step towards peace and prosperity for us all.

Manufacturing was on the rise making their owners quite rich while the everyday worker struggled with long hours and not enough pay. The work was hard and the conditions were poor. In the 1830's and 1840's, groups were forming with their efforts aimed at shortening the work day to ten hours. But, it wasn't until the 1850's that unions were starting to organize in an effort to bring some balance of the oppressed worker with the elite favored owners.

While this was happening, where was the individual in relation to group influence and its control? Again we are getting into a consciousness that our forefathers had warned us against. As more conflict is injected into our consciousness, more control is needed. A minority interest, as a group or faction, gradually assumes more power and control to serve their own special interests, greatly distancing the individual and his/her participation.

The withholding of information from the citizen and the preoccupation in daily life for survival create an ignorant citizen and an ignorant society. Democracy erodes.

When groups were gradually allowed to grow and empower, their influence on society life, coupled with the reduction in individual understanding and information, the wider the gap became between government and its people. The more ignorant the people were, the less they would participate in their governance. The doors were opening wider and wider making it easier for these groups to control the economics of our nation and influence its political leaders. The era of capitalism was coming and we were its cheerleaders. Government and Business were partners. It was another invitation towards despotic ways.

Although the northern states were now Free states, slavery was still an issue and not abolished until after the Civil War in 1865. The face of slavery was changing and with the new wave of industrialism, the seeds had been planted for a new kind of slavery....economic slavery.

The Civil War was near. But, let's address war. Since forming, our young nation had been involved in the Napoleonic Wars (1803 to 1815), the War of 1812 with England, the Mexican Cession in 1845, the Civil War (1861 to 1865), constantly with the Indians until Wounded Knee December 29, 1890, and let's not forget the Spanish American War in 1898. Wow! What a century!

Violence is the part of our humanness or human consciousness that our forefathers talked about. Peace,
Safety, Liberty and Happiness for all people are interwoven throughout our Constitution. Our forefathers
knew that no set of laws could legislate our humanness
and our values preserving our freedom. Violence and
peace are in conflict, deeply embedded. They are choices
of the heart. Liberty, its freedom and happiness, comes
from the heart. The hearts of the people must speak and
beat loudly to the same tune.

Unless our hearts are at peace, violence will be ram-
pant. Unless our hearts know prosperity, greed will create
large gaps between the haves' and have not's', encourag-
ing oppression. Unless our hearts value the individual, all
individuals equally, groups, parties or factions will always
rule and serve their own special interests at the expense of
the many. Unless our hearts value the "I" in "We", we are
fated to a path of some sort of despotism.

Our forefathers knew that information must freely
flow to the people. They know that understanding and
the participation of the individual must be encouraged
and be easy. They knew that if the passion in the hearts of
the people were kept alive that the people would be the
balance needed.

The Civil War was over! We were definitely in a period
of change. Question??? Did we really learn from the Civil
War and what was it? Let's see! A lot of lives were lost

and a lot of families, their homesteads and their way of life destroyed. Four million slaves were now free without any legislation regarding their freedom and citizenship. This has led to over a century of bitter civil rights conflicts. Yes! The union was preserved, but it still had a price to pay among chaos. Did we really come together or continue to divide? What do our hearts say?

Although reconstruction was slow and bitterness was still brewing between the 'northerners' and the 'southerners', a lot was being done to finish out the century and begin the next. America was on the move.

Our lands west of the Mississippi River were being developed. The Indians were being eliminated, riches, such as silver were discovered, the railroad had joined our two shores in 1869, and the industrial revolution was transforming our American society.

The greatest effect centered on industrialization and where it was leading us. We were moving. Our American exports had been steadily rising and jumped from 858 million in 1870 to 1.4 billion in 1900. In 1879, Marshall Field opened our first department store. Big business was on the move. Unions were growing and gaining power. John D. Rockefeller had formed Standard Oil in 1882 and controlled 90% of the American oil production. Monopolies grew and between 1895 and 1904 an "Era of Mergers" was happening, allowing a single holding company to control 60% of the production of 50 companies. This growth was very attractive to people from all parts of the world. Immigration was at an all time high. Our cities were growing and by 1880, 28% of the people had been urbanized. By 1910, the cities had grown even more; 46% of the population was urbanized.

So where does this take us just prior to World War I? We have three major movements happening at the same time; separate, yet closely related.

One was our continual expansion into our new territories. Violence was dominate. The need for goods, American goods, was rapidly growing. And yes, people, many people were in great demand.

The second was industrialization. Not only had our exports vastly increased, but our once unsettled lands were in dire need of manufactured goods. American business was in demand and its owners were getting rich. American business was given a free hand. With little governmental interference the elite few were gaining a lot of power over the masses. The gap in classes was widening. The government seemed to turn a blind eye, so the people turned to the unions to balance their rights and close this gap. The growth of our cities was adding to this gap.

The third factor was our huge wave of immigration that helped crowd our cities. When people are crowded into a dense space; money, food and space begin to oppress their freedom. A new kind of slavery begins to grow. The seeds had been planted and 'economic slavery' was sprouting new buds.

In short, our nation was being divided religiously, socially, politically and economically. If you look at history, not many years go by without some involvement in war, and World War I was coming. War has always united us, bringing with it a false sense of security. Patriotism and the hope of peace and prosperity begins to rise again. Violence seems to incite passion.

Now, I realize that some wars are, or seem to be, unavoidable. We have been attacked before and have responded. We must note. War is profitable for the rich, specifically for big business, while you the people, the masses, pay the price with your lives and your tax money. You pay for the war while a handful of people and their companies profit. At the root of war is **violence, power** and **money.** This is very true today. Iraq is an excellent example. We will elaborate on this later in this section when we talk of government today, its democracy, its capitalism and the nine foot rope theory we practice.

Remember, just before World War I, we were using telephones, just starting to drive cars, flying airplanes. And in 1915, the motion picture industry had started. Our technology had changed quite rapidly so that by the time we entered the war, we had risen to new levels of destruction. All.... in the name of freedom.

So what was life like after our victory celebration?
Well, we must have drank a lot of intoxicating alcohol,
because in 1919, the 18th Amendment was added to our
Constitution and not repealed until 1933. The greatest
influence came from a group known as the Anti-Saloon
League. I emphasis group here; obviously the people did
not agree. In the twenties, bootleg alcohol was the second
largest industry next to the automobile production.

The "Roaring Twenties" were quite unique. In 1920,
women were given the right to vote, they were wearing
their dresses shorter, their hair was shorter, they were
dancing in clubs, drinking alcohol and smoking cigarettes.
Organized crime was growing richer and richer due to
prohibition. Wow! Wild times....crime really does pay. To
add to this unrest, the Klan had risen to new heights of
hatred. We ended the twenties on a bang; the stock mar-
ket crashed and the depression began. The "New Deal"
had limited effects on our depressed economy. Our economy was not able to rebound until the start of World War
II. Yes, war again, but this time we were attacked on December 7, 1941, at Pearl Harbor. We had no choice. In
1945, World War II ended...another big bang. This time
it was nuclear technology; a threat that is still with us today. Once again, our first use of new technology was used
for destruction. Is fear really the 'mother of invention'?

The 'Cold War' now blanketed the world. More walls
of separation were erected. Fear ruled.

The economy in the 1950's and 1960's was strong. The average buying power had increased 20% with unemployment dropping to about 5%. Television was our new communication.

Civil rights was a central issue in the 1950's and 1960's centering on Martin Luther King, a man whose passion had stirred the country. Much legislation was passed that helped to open the doors of equality. However, equality has to be in the hearts (consciousness) of the people before it will actually show up in our society.

Although in the 1950's, we had the Korean War and in the 1960's, we had the Vietnam War (1963 to 1973) and the Cuban Missile Crisis in 1962, it was a productive time for the people. We had the space program. We had Lyndon B. Johnson's "Great Society" where the emphasis was on the economy, education and medical care. Also, we were dealing with civil and equal rights. It was an era of flower children, long hair, drugs, sex, and protests. Yes, there were some instances that we would rather not to have happened, but the people were speaking out, the masses were participating in their own destiny. Change was happening and the people, the individuals, were at the core of the changes.

The worst thing, by far, in relation to democracy was McCarthyism. Senator McCarthy chaired a special committee in 1952 to deal with Communist Sympathizers. He used communist's tactics to fight Communism. He used fear and badgered the witnesses culminating in the destruction of many public careers. Even though he didn't produce evidence that a single federal employee had communist ties, the hearings went on until 1954. Our government allowed our citizens to be unduly and publicly oppressed. It wasn't until 1954, when McCarthy overreached himself by attacking President Dwight D. Eisenhower, Secretary of State Robert Stevens and the Armed Services that action was taken. The Army vs. McCarthy hearings took place destroying McCarthy's public image.

One must ask; how long would this have been allowed to go on? Our government didn't stop this attack on its people. Where was the "Bill of Rights"? The action stopped only when our President and our government was attacked. Once again a small group was able to serve its own special interests and feed its personal power at the expense of democracy and the individual. This is a major point that our forefathers warned us about and has repeated itself time and time again. The integrity of the people and its administrators is the solution. Civil society and its organizations are today's answer. This will be discussed in Section III.

To round out the 1960's, John F. Kennedy, Martin Luther King and Robert Kennedy were assassinated. Richard Nixon was barely elected and in 1969, the microprocessor was developed.

The 1970's were noted for its recession. Both President Ford and President Carter had to deal with inflation. Our industrial output was lower and our unemployment was higher. Individual buying power was much lower as inflation rose to 13.4%. On the political front, the Watergate scandal tarnished the integrity of our political system of government. The Arab oil embargo in 1973 ended our economic boom as well as complicating world relations.

The 1980's were noted for the end of the Cold War. This was the Reagan era and moderately uneventful. On a positive note, our economy was improving.

In the early 1990's, under President George Bush, our economy was shaky with the census bureau reporting that 14.2% of the people lived in poverty. George Bush was noted for 'Operation Desert Storm'. It was a short war and as far as war goes, it was the least costly in terms of lives and destruction. This was actually a defensive action with the sole purpose of keeping Iraq within their own borders.

Now, I'm not endorsing war and neither did our forefathers. They were against aggressive war on our part, but realized that the rest of the world may involve us in a military action. I think our forefathers would agree that this war was in alignment with their intent and was intelligently handled.

President Clinton (1993 to 2001) took us to the 21st century by successfully concentrating on domestic issues. These were relatively good years, in some ways.

B: DEMOCRACY TODAY

Note: *There are things in this section that are repeated several times. Each time is a little different. Remember, this format is that of a talk. Repetition is common in a talk format. There are many reasons for this. This helps to merge both you the listener and you the speaker as one. You are both at the same time. Its you…your story that arises and weaves between the lines, giving them meaning….your meaning.*

It is our history, our people and our leaders that have steered the "Good Ship Democracy" to where it has arrived today. All of us occupy this landing pad. It is not a 'good' pad or a 'bad' pad, but it is our pad. We the people are directly responsible for its NOW destiny. We are the launchers. Where do we choose to go? More importantly, how are we going to proceed and what guiding principles are we going to proceed by? One must ask? How important is our Constitution, the Bill of Rights and the democracy it represents? How important are we, each and every one of us? Are we willing to do what it takes? It is no secret that we are a strong people when we choose to be. Do we choose? Do we dare to be? That is an important question, because ideas and ideals without action go nowhere and mean nothing. Nothing, nothing will happen unless we make it happen.

First, we must look at where we are today. Closely and honestly look. We have to be clear. Truth is clarity. Lack of truth is what's painful. Lack of truth is like looking at life through a fog. It's hard moving and who knows where you end up. Truth is clear. The mere seeing in clarity creates a solution. It's automatic. The answer emerges from the question. That is, the answer is as clear, empowering and effective, as one sees. Truth not only sets us free, but promotes a lasting freedom.

So let's look at the facts of where we are today. These are just the facts of truth. If we don't see life as it truly is, we won't be able to make the necessary changes to reshape our destiny as we choose.

Let's start where we left off. The 'Clinton Years' were good years. We were able to balance our spending and improve the economy at the same time. Politically it was a struggle between the parties. It seems the parties, not the people, were more important. As a result, even though President Clinton introduced a healthcare program, nothing was accomplished. The parties could not agree. Perhaps, if there were no parties, we would have a healthcare program today? It seemed that it was more important to 'get Bill' instead. A golden opportunity was allowed to pass. Another case of "we" the party and not "we the people". **OUTRAGEOUS!**

What did we the people do? We took these irresponsible, ineffective (to me), non-patriotic representatives and re-elected many of them. Were we too comfortable? Do we not care? They work for us! We pay them! They are responsible to support all of us, represent our interests and not theirs. How did they vote? Did they vote for their party or the people? **Find out! Take action!** We need to be responsible and vote for people to represent us....all of us. They take an oath to do this. Hold them to it.

It's the 21st century. We are off and running. We had a situation in the last two elections where there were serious discrepancies in the vote tallying, to the point where the Supreme Court had to get involved to make a ruling. Many people feel that we have a non-elected president. You decide for yourself! Where are our 'checks and balances' in our vote tallying system? This is not democracy as we want it to be! This would never have happened if "we the people" fully participated in our government both individually and through Civil Society Organizations. One issue should never be strong enough to decide an election. This is a sign of special interest groups. We need to elect candidates that represent all of the people and all of their interests. What I find interesting and insightful is that our current politics allows this. Here we elect (or non -elect) a candidate on non-issues. When is gay marriage more important than healthcare or education? We talk about gun control (NRA) and abortion and not about energy, the environment or housing. Why? Why did we elect these people and what did we vote for anyway? Are we informed voters? If by chance that you happen to be informed to any degree, it's not because of the candidates. At this rate, we might as well pick a name out of a hat. It couldn't be any worse. Actually, it might even be better. A sad case. In a sense, we have a Congress and President without any known credentials. No joke! Most voters know little or nothing about either the candidate or the issues.

Our system of government **fails** to inform the people. An uninformed voter has no representation and won't until he or she demands it. This is why certain individuals and special interest groups are so powerful today.

Onward! Unfortunately, we did have 9/11. Terrible, there is nothing good that can be said here. Yes, there is always something that can be learned, but is this really the way that we choose to learn? No!

We live in a highly technical age where everything moves fast, especially information. Here it took twenty minutes for the President to react (it's on tape) and over one day to respond to the people. Hello....was anybody home? He hid for twenty-four hours....no leader to be found. However, he did show up a couple of days later for a photo opt at ground zero. Politics? You bet!

Opportunity had struck. Instead of devising an effective plan to protect our country and its citizens as well as deal with terrorism; we chose, our government that is chose, to lie to its people and their representatives in

Congress, so we could go to war. Fear spoke. We were told of weapons of mass destruction and of terrorist ties. None of this was true (proven fact). As a result, over three thousand soldiers and over 700,000 Iraqi citizens were sent to their deaths; not to count the thousands and thousands who have been injured along with an entire country destroyed. For what? Oil? Money? You decide, but, answer this question. Who profits and who pays? Democracy in action?

War is a touchy subject and this one has already lasted longer than World War II with no end in sight and no plan to end it. Remember; you were uninformed, the truth was kept from you (hidden) and you were denied your right to participate and choose. A government of the people? Not in this case. This war is expensive (over 500+ billion and rising) and it's your money. Did you have anything to say about this? What did we really learn?

While we are on the subject of money, I want to remind you that we now have, today that is, the largest deficit in the history of our nation. Our manufacturing is now behind Asia and declining steadily. Gas prices are skyrocketing. Do we have an energy policy other than buy more oil? Education is in trouble and drastically slipping. Our borders are open to both people and drugs. Homeland security is an expensive joke. Hurricane Katrina? Well, let's not go there. That's a book in itself. Again I ask? Who profits and who pays?

Alarm! Alarm! Alarm! People wake up and get your head out of the sand! I know that you've heard this before, but, if we don't wake ourselves up and act, nobody else will. They want us asleep. It gives small factions freedom....our freedom. I guarantee you this: If we continue on this path much longer, you will be hard pressed to find the middle class. **It is a fact that the disappearance of the middle class and the disappearance of Democracy go hand in hand.** Do-nothing leaders and people that do nothing about it open the doors to despotism.

We need to pick good people who put the need of the people and this country above all. We need to hold them accountable and set good priorities. They work for us! Together our greatness will reappear.

Who are the key people around our leaders? Where is their allegiance? To the people they are suppose to serve, their country or their leader? Look closely! Aren't they a bunch of ass kissers? If they all owe their jobs to the president and are yes men (women too), then why do we need them? We are spending a lot of wasted money on many voices that are paid to say the same thing.

I know I have mentioned this before, but this is a 180 degree turn away from democracy and the intent of our forefathers and the Constitution. A government of the few....for the few....and by the few is not a government of the people. In today's government, the checks and balances set up in our Constitution have all but disappeared. Our Congress, Executive branch and the Judicial branch work for you. You elect them! We need to hold them accountable. Ask questions and keep badgering them if you must. They owe you.

Our elections have been further complicated in today's world because of the enormous amounts of money it takes to be elected. Because of money, more votes are bought today than ever before. This is wrong and must change. It is not what our forefathers had in mind. They warned us about allowing special interest groups to take over. In today's world 90% or more of our people do not stand a chance of election because of money (this is a fact).

Until this changes, we can still hold our candidates accountable. Ask questions about real issues....your issues. In the last election, gay marriage received more attention than healthcare and education. This is outrageous! As for me, I don't see where gay marriage affects this country (our world) anywhere near as much as healthcare and education. Let's not forget the environment, housing, jobs and energy. I think that it's clear that our candidates won't deal with anymore than they think that they have to. They prefer to spend their time offering us many false promises. Don't let them get away with it! Don't settle for less! You are worth it! It's your money being spent, not theirs.

We need a good business plan based on real issues. We need good, responsible people to lead us, representing our needs. Hold our candidates accountable to a plan and results. We need to take care of now, as well as our kids' futures. Vote for people who are committed to making a difference for the common good.

Is it working? I think that this is a very important question; so important that it should apply to everything that we do. We need to check on what we are doing to see if it's working and how we can improve the results. If you owned a large business, wouldn't you check on your products and procedures? If you found a procedure not working would you continue to use it? If you found your product not working would you make thousands more and expect the problem to be solved? These answers are **No!** And **No!** Our government hasn't learned this; at least they pretend not to anyway. **Outrageous! You bet!**

There are many foreign and domestic matters that we repeatedly throw our money away on. None is more serious than war, because it is no longer just money, it's lives that are lost, lives that are injured and families that are ruined. Your children and my children pay a heavy price.

Did we learn from Korea? No, we went to Vietnam. Did we learn from Vietnam? No, we went to Iraq. Here we are over four years later (longer than World War II) in a no-win war many deaths later, a war that we should never have started (fact) and one with no end in sight (fact), not even a plan in place (fact). Yet, we keep sending more soldiers to die. If this war is such a hot idea; why doesn't the President, Vice President, all the appointed advisors and members of Congress send all of their children to Iraq? Do you think they would risk their children's lives? No way! Outrageous! This whole war is ludicrous. By the way people, who is running this country? Whose country is it? It's yours! You own this country. It doesn't own you! Our Constitution says so.

So much for this. I could go on and on. Need I? I think that we can simplify this easily. Our voice today is limited. Our freedoms are becoming more and more of an illusion. If we truly look with clarity, we would know that today our government is: of the few....for the few...and by the few. Parties, factions and groups have taken over and the individual has been expensed out. **People wake up! Get your head out of the sand!** You are important! You are the heart and pulse of our way of life. Stand up! Let freedom ring again. You, the individual, are what it's all about...the core of democracy is you.

So the question becomes; how can I stand up and make a difference? How important am I? Say this: I am... I am...I am important...my kids are important...my grandkids are important...my life is important...my environment is important...and my world is important. **I matter!!!!!**

This is where the civil society organizations can help the individual express him/herself clearly and freely. Together we make a difference.

The next section shows us where and how the individual and Civil Society Organizations can keep a check on and influence government to be open and responsible to the individual and his/her freedoms.

C: THE INDIVIDUAL & CIVIL SOCIETY ORGANIZATIONS

At this point, I think that we need to discuss briefly one of the major reasons that the erosion of democracy could happen. What makes America different? Why are American traditions different from the rest of the world? Who makes up America? We were the formation of dissatisfied people from a variety of cultures. In fact, we became a melting pot, a blending, open to all cultures of the world. We had no folklore of our own and were too busy building our future to form one. It was a tradition in other cultures around the world to pass down the ways and the wisdom of the people, from grandfather to grandson, from generation to generation, through music, poetry and stories. This kept alive the reason, the purpose and value of life as seen through the individual cultures.

We let this slip away from us. We started a country, a folklore and never took the time or valued the passing down of our ways and wisdom. We did not hold on to the very reason that we came here in the first place. Apparently, we did not value who we were or what we stood for enough. If you don't talk about who you are and where you come from (ancestors), then you lose your interest. Your value disappears and fades into nothing. Then you are that nothing, personified...nothing in reality. There is no importance or value placed in the individual. Let's re-build our folklore, our values, and pass it down to our children, as well as, our future generations. There is nothing more powerful than our rich history, our Constitution, its Bill of Rights, the democracy it represents and the "American Dream".

Civil Society is one way to stimulate this and re-start our story....our American Dream.

Note: Maybe, I have been a little too hard....or have I? You decide! That's the point, isn't it? Participate in thinking....your own thinking and take action. Voice without action goes nowhere. Democracy is, or was, originally about and for the individual. Where is it now? Who does it benefit? Is your voice heard? Can it be? Ask yourself: who pays and who profits? Are you outraged? I am...frankly, I am totally pissed. If you are like me, it's time to stand up for liberty and speak out. Don't settle for less. Remember; it is your country. They work for you. It's; we the people. Remember?

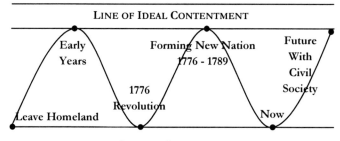

Democracy and Contentment

The diminishment of freedom and the disappearance of the middle class is in direct relation to the degree of oppression. In the early 1600's, the original settlers fled England because of extreme social, political, religious, and economic oppression, causing the elite to separate from the close merging of the middle and poor class. In the early years, the middle and poor classes were close and operated in harmony. As we prospered, the colonies became economically attractive to Mother England. To obtain control, King George III began extreme oppression, leading to the Revolution. Times were again good during the formation of our new government, but as we expanded our borders, the face of democracy slowly changed to Capitalism. So, now the diminishment of freedom and the disappearance of the middle class are at the same degree of oppression as it was when the original settlers left Mother England and during our Revolution. The chart below shows the separation and merging of the classes at each point in our history. When our consciousness moves from the importance of the individual to the importance of a group (a minority one), democracy gives way to Capitalism and despotic ways.

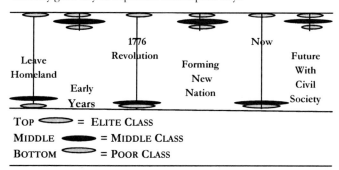

SECTION III

AAAAH! ... THE SOLUTION

AAAAH! ... THE SOLUTION

I know that you probably already have the answer or at least a pretty good idea anyway. That was the purpose of the first two sections of this book. It was meant to provoke your thoughts to interweave between the lines and give them meaning. After all the answer is really simple. It is you, you the individual, each and every one of you. Much of the solution has already been discussed. Just defining the problem gives freedom to the solution. Ask and you shall receive. Yes, the answer is in the question. But, let's spend a little more time together and share our thoughts so that we will be very clear on this. The more we understand the more peaceful our lives will be, the more Life, Liberty, Security and Happiness we will have in our lives. Our forefathers are with us on this, each step of our way.

So let's get started. The first thing that we have to remember is that our country is at its greatest when our Constitution and the Bill of Rights are being used as our forefathers intended. Now Section I covers this, as well as, contains copies of our important documents, letters and addresses at the section's end. Democracy and the various documents are discussed very effectively. However, please read, or re-read them, make notes on points that strike your interest; you will be crystal clear that it's about you, you the individual, each and every individual equally. You are never to be expensed out by special interest groups, parties or factions. This is a government of the people…for the people…and by the people…all the people.

What do we do? Realize your own importance; get involved and vote; elect leaders that will represent you for the common good of all the people. Hold them accountable and responsible for empowering results. Demand that your issues be dealt with. Demand information. Remember, it's your country. You pay them. They work for you…you do not work for them. It's simple! Get involved, set priorities and demand results.

This can be done in one election if we, the people, get involved. Ask questions and demand answers. Be well informed. Hold our leaders and candidates accountable and responsible. Set priorities. Don't settle for less. One election will make the difference and set the trend for Democracy and the American Dream.

Now is important. Now is the future. An effective, empowering, happy, peaceful and loving now is an effective, empowering, happy, peaceful and loving future for our kids. It's simple, the seeds you plant today and how you nurture them are the crop of the future. You are your kid's future…plant well.

Here are the Seven Seeds of Democracy. Number one is to **Realize Your Own Importance.** If you know your importance, you will know my importance and everyone else's importance, too. I can't emphasis this too much.

Our forefathers found you, the individual, to be the key to democracy….its' core. Everything in our Constitution, Bill of Rights and the democracy it represents is about the individual. Why did we declare independence? The individual…the individual. It's simple! If you do not value your importance, democracy won't work. Are you important? Yes!...Yes!...Yes!...and Yes!

The second thing is to **Get Involved.** The only way that change is going to happen is for you to get informed, be knowledgeable and take action. How can you have an input, a say so in your own life, your own destiny, if you are un-informed? Which brings up another question. What do you think of yourself? The more that people value themselves and get involved, the quicker and easier change comes about. It is consciousness that facilitates change. That's right! Consciousness plus action creates your reality.

The third thing is to **Demand Information.** By rights you are entitled to the necessary information…all of the information. Every leader, elected or non-elected representative and government employee is legally bound to furnish you all of the information. It's the law! If you demand information, they will be more careful about what they do with it. A well-informed citizen sets the stage for well-informed decisions. It's the lack of information that makes it easy for politicians to manipulate you. Here again, it's simple. Demand more information and your government will serve you better.

The fourth item on our list is to **Vote.** It doesn't matter how informed you are; if you don't vote, someone else is making the decision for you. The fact is; the fewer people that vote, the easier it is for special interest groups, factions or parties to target certain voters. These voters are loyal and then make up a high percentage of the votes that are cast. The lower the vote, the closer the election and the more likely the one elected will represent a minority that is largely made up of special interests. So, go ahead, don't vote and turn your country over to the special interest groups. In other words; don't vote and give your freedom away.

Of the major republics that hold elections around the world today, the United States has one of the worst voting records. In the last election, only 45% of the eligible voters voted. In Canada, 73% vote and in Australia, 96% vote. The decline in voting is in direct relation to the disappearing of both democracy and the middle class. It's simple! Vote and be **heard** or don't vote and be part of their **herd.**

Number five is to **Elect Leaders**. First of all there is a big difference between a leader and a dictator. A dictator is separate from the group. He owns the group. He controls what the group does for his own benefit. This is scary! To me, it is anyway. As I look at our country today; I'm beginning to see a similarity and I see that the differences, that still keep us a democracy, are slowly slipping away. A **leader** is part of the group. This person steps forward from the group to represent all of the group equally, for the common good. This person keeps a strong focus on the group interest. This person is a creative individual of character who communicates openly and honestly with the people, a man or woman of integrity that is strong, determined and competent. This person inspires the people because he/she touches the heart of the people. This person is the people and the people are of this person. Be choosy. Make sure the people you support and elect care. If they don't, your interest will never be served.

Number six is to **Set Priorities And Define The Issues.** Issues, issues, issues, issues and issues. What is important to you? Do you really want to talk about gay marriage or do you want to talk about healthcare, education and jobs? Do you want to spend three days debating flag burning (your representatives did) or would you rather talk about energy? Do you realize that we have been talking about energy since the sixties and still don't have an energy policy or even a plan in place? Also, you would think that after Bill Clinton put so much effort (years) to establish a healthcare plan that served our country well, Congress would have come up with something better than we have. Actually, we don't have anything. They spent their time shooting the Clinton Plan down and not enough time on a new effective and constructive plan. What's important to our representatives? Where are their priorities? We need to get tough and demand action. Where are your values? Let them know.

Number seven is to **Hold Them Accountable For Their Actions (or lack of action). Hold Them Responsible For The Results.** Ask questions and demand answers, direct, honest and to the point answers. It is outrageous how little Congress accomplishes in our country today. It's even more outrageous that the issues we hold important today are the same ones we held important years and years ago. Our candidates promise us the moon to get elected and then disappear. What do we do? Well, we say congratulations; we know you didn't keep your promises; we know you don't care; but we'll re-elect you anyway. Do you realize how many times these same candidates have been re-elected? How many "do nothing" terms are we going to let them serve? Do we care? If we do, we must hold them accountable and demand results. If they refuse to serve us for our common good, we need to replace them; all of them, if it is necessary. We would be better off electing a brand new Congress (every last one of them) than to re-elect the same mistakes and the same problems that we have today.

Remember that they work for you. You are the boss here. It's your country. Get involved! Set priorities! Make your issues their issues! Demand accountability! Demand answers! Demand results! Demand! Demand! Demand! Don't settle for less!

This is what our forefathers worked so hard to put in place for us. They clearly wanted a better world for their children, their grandchildren, as well as, future generations to come. All we are talking about is just being true to the Constitution, the Bill of Rights, their intention and the democracy it represents. All "we the people" have to do is to be true to this. Speak out! It is your guaranteed right. It is your duty. Patriotism and the true patriot value, support and are true to our Constitution, our Bill of Rights and Democracy as our forefathers intended. Anything else is un-patriotic.

Are you patriotic? Do you value this great country of ours? Do you believe in American Democracy as our forefathers did? These seven things are a good beginning. They are just about you...you being you. Democracy is not just a governance...it is a way of life where you value yourself individually and you value everyone else individually and equally. Greatness is as unlimited as we value the "I" in the "We". When each and every "I" is valued, "We" are unstoppable. 'Be' and 'Dare to Be'...that is the solution. You are the Dream.

HOW DO WE DO THIS?

This part of Section III is about how the person can either individually or as a "Civil Society Organization" participate effectively in democracy, empower and enhance today's society and today's world. It covers ways that we can bring harmony and a common understanding with our leaders, so that we can operate together as one movement for our common good. Solution to today's issues and problems naturally emerge when everyone is well-informed and freely able to participate in some way as much or as little as one chooses. When competition and comparison are eliminated, the obstacles we face daily disappear.

If we love this country and we love its' people, then nothing is impossible and nobody goes wanting. Life flows with a natural ease, if we just let it. Miracles happen if we just get out of their way. Let's take a giant step for mankind, so that all of us can experience our birthright... heaven on earth.

First, let us review what 'Civil Society' is so that we know what a 'Civil Society Organization' must represent.

Civil Society: *A society in which the individual is important and has a full voice in his/her direction; using a system where the value of each individual is united in common cause. 'Life is a gift for all individuals and all individuals are a unique gift to life'. With this at our core, oppression disappears and has no chance of returning.*

A civil society is a strong society, where our economic, religious, social and political interests are balanced for the benefit of all. Our best defense is a debt-free country, a powerful military (non-aggressive...a deterrent) with a harmonious society free to grow and express themselves as they choose, as long as they honor each other's individual freedom and liberty. This is also our best offence.

It is a society based on the premise; "of the people… for the people…and by the people". A system of majority rule, equally representing each individual and not at the expense of the other. In other words; everyone benefits even if they were out voted.

In this way, no group could gain control at the expense of others. Our forefathers were very clear as to the problem of a party (faction or group) system and its being a minority rule. It opens the door to despotism…of the group…for the group…and by the group. When this happens, the individual no longer matters. His/her individual freedom and liberty disappears. A group dictates.

In short, 'Civil Society' represents harmony among its individuals, an equality where it is easy and encouraged for the individual to participate in its affairs with a government "of the people…for the people…and by the people". A government that is based on a democracy guarantees freedom of action and speech of all its people, in all areas, including the religious, social, political and economic phases of societal life.

Individuals united in common cause eliminate the power and danger of group rule and its despotic tendency.

* * * * *

Now there are three things that will come up regularly that need to be addressed by both the individual and civil society organizations, so that the **Seven Seeds of American Democracy** and the individual will grow effectively and empower the "American Dream".

The first is "isms". All *isms* have a commonality, whether it be socialism, Marxism, Darwinism, feminism, pauperism, sexism, racism, Buddhism, terrorism, despotism, activism or capitalism. *Isms* are a minority interest where the interest of a few try to influence the many. Isms are controlling. All of the power and money are in the hands of a very small group at the expense of the many. Look at all of the *isms* and ask; Who benefits and who pays? *Isms* do not consider individual merits. They are an attitude of superiority. Judgment is based on the characteristics of the group. You are the group and are what I (the group) think the group stands for. So as an *ism*, I (the minority or small group) am superior or better than you or the masses. As you can see, this is directly the opposite of democracy, our Constitution and the intent of our forefathers. Our forefathers warned us about the power of groups, factions or parties. There are no *isms* in democracy. All the people are equal. The individual is the core of our system of governance, our consciousness and our way of life.

The second thing is what I call the **Nine-Foot Rope Theory.** This is important! It is a common practice used in politics today. The less involved the people get, the more effectively this practice is implemented. It is a tool of deception. In short, it's like this: I throw you a nine-foot rope to reach you when I know it takes a full ten feet. What am I really doing here? I am making it look like (appear that) I am doing everything that I can to help you or to serve your needs; when in reality, I know it won't either help or serve you. Your needs and my agenda are not the same. I'll look good though. Deception! Since it takes money, a lot of it, to get elected, I end up serving my party and several special interest groups. They end up taking priority over the voters. If I am a good politician, I will give the appearance of serving your issues and needs; when in reality, I don't. Unfortunately, politics has become a con game. Remember that every time you get a nine-foot rope, someone that you don't see, gets a ten-foot one.

Neither one of these two things have to happen if you get involved in the Seven Seeds of Democracy. Become them! This is fool proof! Let the "I" in "We" speak.

The third thing is **"People Wake Up! Get Your Head Out Of The Sand! Look Around! Its Right In Front Of You!"** Now did that get your attention? I hope so. It was meant to. How can I even begin to tell you of how important it is for an alert people? I'm not sure that there are words powerful enough to inspire us to be alert and passionate as to our importance as an individual and as a people. This is not just a catchy and humorous phrase. It is serious! Very serious!

Politicians have known for eons the importance of information. That's why they don't give it to you. Only the informed have a vested interest or a valid opinion. So they keep you un-informed. If you don't know, you won't participate. If you are not part of it, they have an open field to do anything they want. This is the nine foot rope theory in use. Most of the time you come up short and are not aware of it. Information frees you. Lack of information paralyzes you. They want you paralyzed, asleep, numb, in a hypnotic state, a trance or better yet all of these. You are being drugged with empty promises and manipulative words. Anything to side track you....divert your attention. When was the last time that you listened to a politician and were clear on what they really said; what they were really going to do? Did they do it? Did you hold them accountable? Did you demand results? Are they worthy of your vote? If you were asleep, you weren't sure; you don't know. If you were awake, you were sure, very sure and very clear. When you are sure, decisions are easy to make and their results follow just as easily. The individual is the core of democracy. Being there is the key that opens the door. Let freedom ring! An alert citizen will never hold on to a nine-foot rope, will never be at the mercy of an *ism*, nor will they be owned by special interest groups, factions or parties. An alert citizen will live and have, Liberty, Security and Happiness. Wake up people! Dare to be! You are worth it!

Let's review. What is the function of Civil Society Organizations?

♦ To facilitate the Seven Seeds of Democracy.

♦ To keep the information flowing to the people so that they are well-informed.

♦ Make it easy to express themselves.

♦ Keep the issues and the people's needs flowing to our leaders (elected and non-elected).

♦ Hold our leaders responsible for dealing with them.

♦ Make them accountable for the results.

Civil Society Organizations are information centers designed to maintain a flow of information to and from the people. They keep the lines of communication open by providing an open platform of discussion, never allowing an issue to go unanswered or partially answered. This creates an automatic action that demands the manifestation of a result.

Let's take an election and ask what would a Civil Society Organization do? A Civil Society Organization would simply magnify the individual. They ask the same questions and seek the same information that the individual does. As an organization, it accesses the talent of many individuals, making it easier to obtain the needed information. Because it is an organization of individuals, for

individuals and by individuals, it enhances the importance
of communication with our leaders and politicians. This
voice is loud, clear and far-reaching. Our politicians know
that what they do and how they act is being overseen or
monitored. Their actions are going to reach the people.
The message will reach the people. The politicians and
our leaders now have to choose what is it that they want
the people to know. This will keep them accountable for
their actions and responsible for the results. This is society's checks and balances. If the candidate does not answer the questions or address an issue, you will know. In
the past, this was not being done, making it easy for the
candidate to dodge the issue and not be held accountable.
This is a denial of democracy. Our forefathers warned us
about this.

Our political parties don't want you to know anymore
than you have to. Our current elections are about the
party, not the person. Issues are of little importance.
Wake up people! Get your head out of the sand....look
around, the answers are right in front of you! The issues
of today are the same as they were in the sixties. It has
taken us forty years to do nothing about education,
healthcare, the economy or energy. As a matter of fact,
each one of these areas is worse off today than they were
forty years ago. This is not democracy. I don't think they
know what democracy and the individual means. I wonder if they have even read the Constitution with its Bill of

Rights. **With an active Civil Society Organization, this would never have happened.**

Let's take just one of these issues and give it to a Civil Society Organization. How about the energy issue? We have a simple policy; more oil…more oil…more oil. It is the same now, as it was over forty years ago. Where has it taken us? To higher prices for the individual and more profit for the oil companies. After all, our politicians need their money to get elected. Democracy…bought and paid for! What information did the public have? Did we ask; who profits and who pays?

Civil Society Organizations would have said:

1. Energy is an issue and would notify all leaders and candidates.

2. Their views and opinions would be requested.

3. Based on their responses, more questions would be raised.

4. Their responses would be made public. All forms of media would be used, including an accessible web site.

5. There would be more questions and answers, to and from the public and the leaders and the candidates. This process would continue so that the issue would not disappear.

6. A public forum would be held where all of the leaders and candidates would be invited. Any person who declined, would be noted by an empty chair with their name on it. This way, their lack of interest and inaccessibility to the public would be clear.

7. All questions would be asked of all leaders and candidates. All answers would be published in their own words, so that the possibility of prejudicism would not exist.

When all of the information is exposed, along with the various answers, all of the people are served. Democracy is about the individual....all individuals equally. No individual should ever be expensed out or burdened for the benefit of another. The only reason a leader or candidate would withhold information would be to prejudice the results for his/her own special interest or benefit.

By setting up a system of communication that is ministered and flows freely and openly to the people and to the leaders and candidates, we keep our government accountable and responsible for the results. Civil Society Organizations put the "I" back in the "We" and bring importance to our Constitution and the Bill of Rights. It also returns meaning to democracy.

A Civil Society Organization must reach the people, reveal their issues and start the flow of information. They are a 'communications center' only. The information must be pure on all sides, complete and unbiased information. In order to make good solid decisions, all information must be expressed; even if it does not support your own view. When all of the information is expressed, a viable solution will emerge. Clear and complete information creates clear and complete solutions.

Civil society is the relationship between the people and the government. It has material, organizational and ideological dimensions. The material approach is largely determined by our economic system of capitalism and the ability of the individual to independently amass capital. The organizational approach focuses on systems that enhance the people's ability to access needed information and easily communicate their issues, questions and opinions to the government (leaders and candidates). The ideological approach keeps focus on the value of the individual, his/her relation to the government and the value, purpose and meaning of our Constitution, Bill of Rights and related documents.

Civil Society Organizations research and reveal information to the public that always promote the growth of democracy. This information and its indicators must be for the benefit of all people equally and must be kept accessible to the people. This is not just limited to our legislation, but also expands the individual's involvement in the selection of our leaders. Democracy must be **open, responsible and accountable.** Politics is about power, and accountability is needed for the responsible use of this power. A knowledgeable, informed and responsible citizenry keeps our government in balance, strengthens our Constitution and its Bill of Rights and helps enhance a pure American Democracy.

Civil Society Organizations create and facilitate forums where our politicians and our leaders listen to public opinion, account for the popular will, become answerable to the peoples decisions and defer to the people's demands. Our political system must be kept fair and balanced so that the very bottom is equal to the top. A government of the people...for the people...and by the people; all of the people, equally, and not at the expense of any. The social, economic and political phases of society must be linked, so that the weakest of voices can be heard. Civil Society Organizations are the peoples megaphone. If the people don't speak, our government won't or can't listen.

You, the individual, are the legitimate voice of politics, government and democracy. We must have a just and accountable government in order to have an equitable economy, as well as, **freedom, liberty, happiness and safety.** Without Civil Society Organizations, our leaders' personal interests will be exploited at the expense of the individual or the public. History clearly shows this. Our system is money driven and our current leaders owe their allegiance to the money holder that backed them. Our forefathers clearly warned us of this. Without the individual at the core of democracy, **despotism** takes over. Political change is necessary, will be there, and must reflect the will of the people. You, the individual, must exert pressure on our leaders and their governance. Your economic and social improvement will be in direct relation to your participation in your society and its political affairs. There is no reason why everyone can't be educated and have a reasonable and healthy existence. **Empowered people make empowered decisions and live empowered lives.**

The key words here are: understanding, participating, accountability and responsibility. Demand! Demand! Demand! Don't accept less! You are worth it!

Temporary fixes are our current government's way of doing things and are backed by special interest groups. They are pacifiers used to avoid changes and citizen involvement. Special interest groups lose power when public involvement increases, also a better understanding occurs and the public economy improves. Empowerment! Empowerment! Empowerment! Remember, your leaders and your government work for you, you don't work for them.

Are you on the outside? Why? Do you care that eight out of the ten Bill of Rights our forefathers held so dear are being blatantly violated today? What do you really value? Who are you? Are you worth it? Are you part of the "We" in the "We am the dream"? I leave it open for you to decide. After all, it is about "you" and you have the last word. When you do decide, let it ring loud and clear from the center of your heart. Let it flow freely through all of your being and radiate its light…a beacon for all to see.

EPILOGUE

AND

OPEN LETTER

WE ARE THE DREAM

Kiss the spirit and it comes alive as you...the dream lives...for you are the dream and wow, what a dream. In theory, this is a one word book: "YOU". So how do you make a one word book understood and still simple? The key is to understand, know your truth and dare to be. You are important. You are valuable. You are part of the "We"...the core of democracy. When you participate and speak; freedom, liberty, happiness and safety live. These four things are of great value and are at our core. They will always elude us as long as we link them up with violence.

If we continue to listen to our leaders and continue to let them run our country, there will be no country. So far, every time we speak of peace, we get violent. The price is high and our way of life has eroded to the point that we are worse off than we were forty years ago. People today know very little about our government. Ask around and see for yourself how many people or actually, how few people have read the Constitution and the Bill of Rights. They actually think that we are a democracy, when in fact, we are a capitalistic nation. Democracy, now empty words, has been reduced to the right to vote. Vote for hand-picked candidates, that is. Our choices are dictated to us, as is our daily lifestyle. The decline in the middle class is in direct relation to the erosion of democracy and freedom.

If you look closely, we have very little say so about anything. Oh, the Constitution says that we do, but the information is kept from us. You see, everything is so complicated that we can't access it. We can't even have access to our leaders. These are the seeds that we have planted for our kids' future. Tomorrow builds on today, and today it is getting harder and harder to see a glimpse of freedom. The freedom, liberty, happiness and safety that are cornerstones of democracy, put in place by our forefathers, have all but crumbled into nothing. Is our country, our proud nation, now built on sand? How long do you really think it can last in these times of uncertainty? Years ago, we found what we were looking for and today we must discover it again before it is too late. Is it too late? Can we transform our world into the paradise it was meant to be? Can we re-spell violence into peace? Yes! Yes! Yes!...we sure can! We did it once and we can do it again. This time England is not our enemy. We are our own enemy.

It's amazing how much power "we the people" have when enough of us stand in our truth. In the face of adversity, the highest courage is to be yourself. Dare to be! Choose right over wrong, ethics over convenience and above all, truth over popularity. Your life, as well as all of our lives, depends on this. Look forward. We are at a fork in the road. Take the path of integrity and remember, there is never a wrong time to do the right thing.

Kiss the same spirit that freed us a long time ago. God to God…from heart to hero. Remember what is being kissed and who is kissing it. Unite spirit with democracy and create a civil society. Dare to be it! You deserve it! You are worth it! You can respect the individual and the whole at the same time. Your consciousness, respect, and harmony is a perfect blend that leads us forward into the American Dream as a true democracy. This is not a compromise. It is a way of life, a consciousness, where we can prosper and all can benefit equally. Our greatness is the heart of the people. Democracy as it was intended to be and oppression cannot co-exist at the same time. Open your heart…be your greatness and listen. The answers are in you. You are its heartbeat. Let it speak for you, as you. Let it pulse through your veins and release its power, a new vitality for all to be. Your country needs you. Do you believe that you are worth it? Are you strong enough? Are you important? You bet you are! You are absolutely divine. Divine Grace is alive as our way of life.

"We the people" want peace. Democracy is about peace. In fact, the vast majority of the world wants peace and prosperity. It's only a few who choose turmoil and chaos and want to control the rest of us, our way of life and our being for their own personal gain. The power has always been in the masses. When the hearts of the people speak, the tyrants have no choice but to listen. Look how powerful our revolution was! On the surface, it looked like we were doomed to a life of oppression, but the heart of the people spoke (aren't you glad it did?). We were free. In India, Gandhi united the hearts of the people. Once again, the power of peace spoke. India was free. Free to choose their way of life. Peace will always overcome tyrants, because in the hearts of the people are peace, and when united in common cause, it cannot and will not be defeated. History reinforces this truth, this undisputable fact. Again, your consciousness, plus your action, creates your reality.

The truth is! Or let's say, truth's teachings are: as you think...so you are! What you focus on becomes real. The heart-mind connection is our power. And when all of us, each and every one of us, are important, stand in their truth and act for the common good, we are unstoppable. Miracles happen and the American Dream unfolds and emerges to a new greatness.

Let the truth be known!
We have risen!
We are the Dream...

AN OPEN LETTER TO OUR LEADERS

You spoke of things as if you know a truth, like you had an inside track that we didn't or weren't able to share. We believed. Our faith embraced you, cheered you on. We lifted you on our shoulders and entrusted you to lead us onward to our destiny. We believed. We knew. Apparently, you didn't. Words so eloquently uttered disappeared into nothing. Promises so passionately made, were no more than hot air. Sincerity without heart. We were careless and you could care less…about us anyway.

We are awakened as we see that the pockets of a few are lined and full as we pay. Pay! Pay! Pay with our lives. Pay with our hard-earned money. Pay with our souls.

Enough! Enough! Enough! No more will we surrender blindly to your wishes. We rise! A new day has come!…An awakening occurs! You work for us…We don't work for you. The Almighty Spirit that flows through us all cannot be silenced! You will listen! You will serve or you will not lead! Our path is the promise land and not your slaughter house. We are not your robots and will not be cloned. The American Dream lives in the hearts of all the people. Each and every one of us is important. Our Constitution, our Bill of Rights and the democracy it represents openly and clearly demands this. We are now involved and change will happen. It's our country, it's our future and we are its destiny. We will learn. We will understand. We will be informed and we will vote. We will elect leaders...true leaders, who care for the common good of all mankind. Leaders who are creative, have integrity, that communicate openly and honestly with the people. Priorities will be set and issues will be defined. Our issues will be dealt with completely. You will be held accountable for your actions and responsible for the results. Our country, our way of life is only as effective, as empowering, as good as the consciousness of the people. The "I" in the "We" speaks. Silence and passivity are no longer an option. **We -- each and every one of us -- are the Dream.**

"We hold these truths to be self evident..."

"Of the people...for the people...and by the people..."

REFERENCES:

THE DECLARATION OF INDEPENDENCE And OTHER GREAT DOCUMENTS OF AMERICAN HISTORY, 1775-1865

Edited by John Graeton
Dover Thrift Editions
Copyright © 2000 Dover Publications Inc.
31 East 2nd St., Mineola, NY 11501

AMERICAN HISTORY — MINIPEDIA

Published 2005 – General Editor, Rana K. Williamsom, Ph.D.
Parragon Publishing – Queen Street House
4 Queen Street
Bath BA1 1HE, U.K.

WHERE HAVE ALL THE LEADERS GONE?

Lee Iacocca with Cathrine Whitney
Copyright © 2007 by Lee Iancocca and Associates, Inc.
A California Corp.
Scribner – A division of Simon and Schuster, Inc.
1230 Avenue of the Americas
New York, NY 10020

9 780981 868806